The Essential Community: Local Government in the Year 2000

The future influences the present just as much as the past.

Friedrich Nietzsche

Municipal Management Series

The Essential Community: Local Government in the Year 2000

Laurence Rutter
for the
ICMA Committee on
Future Horizons of the Profession

George R. Schrader, Chairman

International
City
Management
Association

**Cover photograph by
Kem Kaminsky/UNIPHOTO**

Library of Congress Cataloging in Publication Data
Rutter, Laurence, 1943–
    The essential community.
    (Municipal management series)
    Bibliography: p.
    1. Local government. 2. International City
Management Association. I. Schrader, George R.,
1931–   joint author. II. Title.
III. Series.
JS67.R87   352   80-16901
ISBN 0-87326-994-2

Printed in the United States of America.

Contents

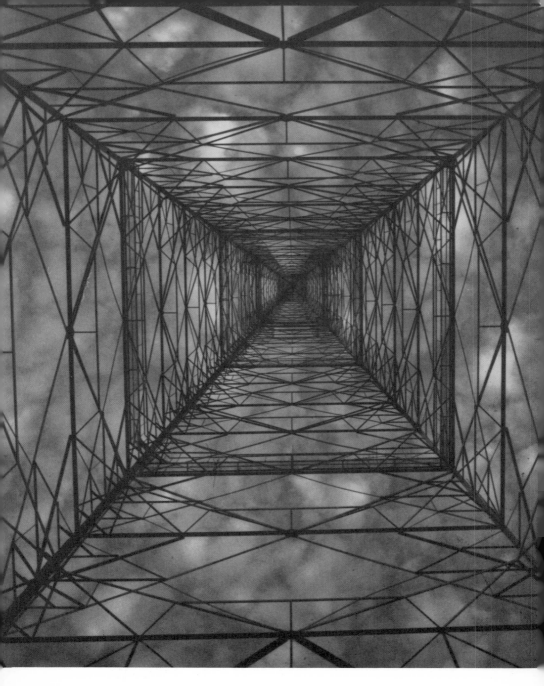

Every cause produces more than one effect.

Herbert Spencer

Welcome to the year 2000

Welcome to the year 2000. Life is better, but not that much different from the way it was in 1979. People appear well dressed, even though the fashions are outlandish—ugly, really. People appear well fed; the stores are stocked with all kinds of goods. Many are driving small automobiles, but there also are a lot of oddly shaped buses. Homes are well cared for, by and large, but some of them are unusual shapes and sizes.

There are all types of people on the streets, men and women, blacks, whites, and Hispanics. There are not many children, but a number of gray-haired people stroll along the pavements.

An aerial view shows that the area is built up as far as the eye can see. Center city appears to be much as it was in 1979, but there also are dense areas in the suburbs. Development is intense around those areas, just as it is near the expressways and mass transit lines.

By now 1984 is long ago and far away. Technology has advanced: overhead wires are almost gone; few homes have television antennas; the cars are small and make very little noise; a few of the video screens found in homes and offices are broadcasting computer printouts rather than TV programs. Both homes and office buildings are built differently; miniature solar panels are on their roofs, and the windows are smaller. The houses are built on smaller lots. Some houses are built underground!

The metropolitan area's local government office building is a modest place, equipped with numerous energy-saving devices. It is a showcase of technology: solar panels; computer-controlled lighting, heating, and cooling systems; and laser-assisted lighting. Video display terminals are on every-one's desks, and people are communicating with each other through these screens by typing messages back and forth.

The council chamber is a large, well-lit auditorium, ringed with miniature TV cameras. There is no throne-like council bench, but there is a series of comfortable lounge chairs for the council and manager.

"Welcome. I am Jennifer Stene, the city coordinator." A talk on the administration of the city will be given by its top professional administrator, a forty-five-year-old veteran of local government administration who has served two other cities and one county.

"The job of 'coordinator' is similar to the job of a city manager or administrator twenty years ago," she explains. "Names change over the years, but the job is very much the same." One of the few differences is that as coordinator, she spends most of her time with the council and community leaders. She is the broker among the various political and social groups in town, and her assistant actually manages the community on a day-to-day basis.

Coordinator Stene talks about the city. "We are one of about forty jurisdictions in this area. I suppose that is about the same number as existed twenty years ago. The major difference is that our mayor is part of the Metropolitan Assembly, a very powerful decision-making body. It costs us quite a bit to belong to the assembly, but we cannot afford not to belong.

"Our city also functions at the neighborhood level. That is where everything comes together: police, fire, collection of trash, water and sewer services, recreation, land use, and so on. All are directed toward the essential community at the neighborhood level. We have long since decentralized the administration of these services, and a fair amount of the policy leadership, to that level."

Cable television is a major feature of the essential community life. "All of our zoning decisions are aired first on CATV, so we get some very solid feedback from our citizens. Our studio and the computer tie-in are fantastic; the system gives us invaluable information about public views on major decisions. The system is not controlled by the city, though, and citizens' groups have direct access to it any time they want to use it."

Some of the problems confronting communities in the year 2000 are the same as those that existed in 1979. "We are still trying to keep down the level and cost of services. We really have not gone far beyond the kinds of things that local governments did twenty years ago. The city's public service corporation provides most of our essential service delivery—especially since we receive very little money from the central, or what was once called the federal, government.

"It is a bit laborious to channel so much of our budget through our public service corporation, whose director the council and I appoint. We would like to do a number of things if we had more money, but if we spend beyond our tax revenues, we try to use local private-sector sources. Many public service projects are funded solely by local businesses and other private organizations, a process that has given us some freedom from central control."

This city in 2000 devotes a lot of attention to the demand for services. "We try to keep demand at a minimum by helping people help themselves. We rent equipment to neighborhood groups so they can do their own tree trimming, street cleaning, or whatever. We also try to price services close to the market level, so that we are sure people receive basic services at a modest price. Additional services, such as trash pickup twice a week, cost more. Most neighborhoods have trash pickup only once a week.

"Prior to coming to this city, I was an administrator in three other places. Like most of my professional colleagues, I stay in any one place about five years. My employment contract will be renegotiated next year when I receive a full evaluation. I have been in this city for four years, so it will probably be renewed for another year. After that I will take a six-month sabbatical, a break that was part of my agreement with the city.

"During my sabbatical I plan to hone some of my skills. I am interested in an intensive course in negotiation being offered by LEMA, the Local Executive Management Association, formerly known as ICMA. So much of my job depends on my ability to negotiate well that I feel I need some refresher courses.

"It is not a question of acquiring more technical knowledge. That's why we have management technicians; our financial coordinator is one of the best; our corporate planner is superb; and the personnel and public works people know their fields.

"My job is to know how to use what they know. I help the council make sense of this technical information . . . to translate it into terms that they and the citizens can understand.

"Too much technical information without the ability to use it reduces its effectiveness. I am really a translator, a broker, a negotiator. I think my title says it best. Coordinator."

The year 2000 is inviting. We can hardly wait.

Men come together in cities in order to live: they remain together in order to live the good life.

Aristotle

Where this book is going

Almost everything that we do that is worth doing is done in the first place in the mind's eye.

J. Bronowski

We are about to embark on a journey through the mind's eye—a journey over the next two decades toward the horizon of time. The pathfinders for our trip are a group of professional local government administrators and their associates who spent a year and a half pooling their imaginations and projecting the future of local government.

This effort was the task of the Committee on Future Horizons of the International City Management Association. Thirty-three committee members peered ahead to the year 2000 to see how local government would be managed in the future. The committee wanted to know how cities, counties, and councils of governments (COGs) will cope over the next twenty years, how the role of the local government administrator will evolve as changes occur, and how best to prepare for these changes.

A healthy skeptic might well ask why we bother looking so far ahead when we have enough to keep us busy right now. Fires need to be fought today. The garbage will rot if not collected now. Immediate problems need immediate solutions. Our days are already filled with complex relations, problems, and prospects.

The reason we look ahead is that the future is all that remains. As Charles F. Kettering wrote, the future is important "because we will have to spend the rest of our lives there." The future of every city, county, or COG is where we are likely to spend our lives as citizens and administrators. The future is all we have to work with as we attempt to improve our society, our country, and our communities.

Another reason the future cannot be ignored is that it creeps up on us unexpectedly. Twenty years seems a vast distance to travel; yet in fact it is a very short distance and one that is traversed quickly by local governments. It takes five to seven years to plan, design, and build a city hall; a major water system cannot be built in less than twelve years; and major transit systems such as those in San Francisco, Atlanta, and Washington, D.C., can take a full twenty years to complete. These services are provided by local governments—the cities, counties, and COGs—and make possible the quality of living we all enjoy.

Looking into the future is important for still another reason—to avoid making mistakes. Very little has been done to look into the future of local governments, and in general urbanists have been poor futurists.

The record of failures to anticipate local government trends has been disheartening:

No one seems to have predicted the effect that federally subsidized mortgages for new homes in the suburbs and the interstate highway system might have on what the National League of Cities has called "urban conservation."

Just a few years ago current wisdom dictated that all jurisdictions should tear up their streetcar tracks and sell the cars to Mexico. Today "light rail transit" is the rage.

A decade ago we were still building schools feverishly. Today, with equal fervor, we are closing vacant buildings for want of students.

Not long ago urban redevelopment meant wholesale demolition of older structures. Only recently have some places begun to realize the value of such structures. In fact, some of the most dramatic recent urban revitalizations (such as those in Philadelphia, Baltimore, and Alexandria, Virginia) have taken place in towns that were not ready for urban renewal in the 1950s and could make splendid use of their solid and historically valuable buildings.

The point here is not to exhibit the clarity of 20/20 hindsight; even if we had looked into the future, we would have missed some of these trends. The point is that we would have spotted others before it was too late. The point is that no one really looked.

THE PERSPECTIVE OF THIS BOOK

The institution of local government is the perspective from which *The Essential Community* is written. It is a broad and useful perspective—one to which most members of the Committee on Future Horizons have devoted their professional careers. The administration of local government is guided by annual budgets; paid for by property taxes and other revenues; directed by elected officials; staffed by police officers, firefighters, and other public service workers; and symbolized by the city hall or county courthouse. It is an intricate and complex field; yet it is the public's work. The public—through elected officials, boards and commissions, and many types of governmental processes—decides what a local government will do.

The committee might have considered other perspectives for viewing the future of local government. Demographic, sociological, geographical, and even psychological viewpoints add important dimensions to future projections. The urban development policies of a federal, or central, government provide another perspective. Viewing the neighborhood as an institution and the urban areas served by local governments as economic systems are two additional ways to look toward the year 2000.

All of these perspectives are valid. If viewed together, they would provide a complex, rich, ambitious mosaic. It would, however, have been a mosaic beyond the resources of the committee, and it would have taken much more space to present the results of such an undertaking than this book allows. The committee is satisfied that its perspective of local government—this view and the committee's interpretations of its findings—gives citizens a realistic chance to change the nature and quality of their lives in this community setting.

COMMITTEE VALUES

Every vision of the future is a prism—altered by the values of the viewer. The future of local government will be affected by the values of today. Thus the members of the committee examined their values and concluded that they believed in the following:

1. Representative democracy. Representative institutions such as Congress, state legislatures, and local councils most effectively represent the democratic spirit. Elected officials work best when they are tuned in to what their constituents want and need. They provide the most expedient and equitable way to resolve social conflicts within communities.
2. Local government. Cities, counties, and COGs offer essential direct

services to citizens, touch citizens most directly, and serve as the best forum for expression of political needs. A dependent or weak local government means a dependent and powerless citizenry.

3. Equity. The concept of equity is an ideal for the future. Although tight budgets, modest growth, shifting populations, and political frustrations generally dilute the concept of equity, the committee believes that local governments must strive continually to achieve equitable delivery of services.

4. The limits of government. Governmental services are *limited*. People should not expect the government to serve their needs indefinitely or without limit. A free people are those who are only modestly dependent on government, who want to and can help themselves, and who patronize healthy private and quasi-private sectors.

The Essential Community was written to show elected officials, citizens, and students of local government how to look toward the future with more clarity than their predecessors. It is an invitation to look beyond today's local problems and to help anticipate and build possible futures. This book is intended to clarify choices so that we can enhance the communities of tomorrow.

Part 1

Urban managers as futurists

Looking to the future

If you do not think about the future, you cannot have one.

John Galsworthy

Urban
managers as
futurists

Urban administrators as futurists are responsible for anticipatory management. They should explore the future in terms of projections and alternatives.
Two sets of disciplines may especially help urban managers as they guide
and implement transitions into the future: those of futures specialists, and
those of public leadership experience.

FUTURES STUDIES

Futures studies do not truly constitute a discipline; they do make up a
relatively new field which employs several existing forecasting methods.
Some of these are disciplined; others are as yet rudimentary in approach.

Exploratory forecasting methods are most frequently used by futurists,
and the ICMA committee relied on these. In most common use long before
contemporary futurism came into vogue are extrapolative methods such as
growth and trend curves which are used regularly in annual government
reports. Explanatory methods such as correlation analysis, study of precur-
sor events or indicators, and construction of causal models are also widely
employed. Conceptual matrices and futures scenarios such as those used
by the ICMA committee are also commonly used in futures studies.

Normative forecasting methods employed by futurists commonly include morphological models, relevance trees, and mission flow diagrams.
All are conceptually simple, but securing and analyzing the information may
not be simple.

Tools often used by futurists in exploratory or normative forecasting
include Delphi (anonymous-group-interaction) methods and computer
simulations, both already common in urban research.

DISCIPLINES OF LEARNING AND ACTION

Other disciplines for urban professionals as futurists are old ones, long tested in public service. They are the classic disciplines of learning and professional action: study of the known and the unknown; awareness of situations and diversity; knowledge of self and of others; and practice of values and processes of democracy. They may serve to create diverse futures from known patterns of the past.

Historians have long understood that history is conditional—that it can be influenced. That fact is the fundamental faith of futures activities. Historians have also understood that even the past cannot be known with certainty—let alone the future. But the classic maxim still holds in large part: the past remains something of a prologue, despite the discontinuities of this age of rapid changes. The past long ago taught scholars and practitioners of government the most basic lesson in futures implementation: that the challenge of successful transition from the present to the future is achievement of reasonable balance between stability and change. This does not deny or reject the possible wisdom of even discontinuous changes; it does suggest the need to balance them, however, with commonly accepted stabilizing forces to preserve the dynamic social fabric of constitutional democracy.

The old conclusions of historians and social scientists are only a tiniest fraction of knowledge from the past. The massiveness of all that is now known surely must produce in an intelligent being some awe at the greater vastness of the unknown. Such humility, born of study or experience, should be a precondition for futurists, lest some of them give illusions of certainty where it does not exist. Such informed humility has long been fundamental to survival as an urban manager, at least, and that is one of the requisites for the job which seems likely to persist into the next century.

The city management movement was born in the era of the "one best way," but, like public administration generally, it has now moved beyond that restricted view conceptually and in practice. *

This change has not involved a rejection of scientific methods, common experience, or shared efforts to improve. Those disciplines remain basic to the profession. They have taught practitioners the necessities of situational knowledge in urban politics and management as well as the value of diversity. The contingency management approaches which have been learned are well suited to implementing transitions into unknown futures.

Learning about self and about others is essential to understanding of the fundamental democratic value of human dignity. It is a searching process, like life itself.

It is that process of searching that defines human dignity. It is the sort of dream about which Martin Luther King spoke. Such human dignity is found in the stretching of imagination from past experiences of happiness and despair to new hopes for better futures.

Human dignity as a process of disciplined lifelong searching is but one of the two most basic values of the democratic heritage identified earlier. Rule of law is the other. And, like human dignity, it is defined in Western experience as a vigorous yet humble process of unending inquiry.

It is the searching for reasonableness in public affairs which underlies the processes of constitutional democracy. That is an old formula for governance in the present with a responsible eye to the future. It is a most necessary discipline for desirable futures of urban diversity and democracy.

Source: Excerpted from Chester A. Newland, "Future Images: Urban Diversity and Democracy?" *The Municipal Year Book, 1979* (Washington, D.C.: International City Management Association, 1979), pp. 5–6.

A great flame follows a little spark.

Dante Alighieri

Looking to the future

Futurists are everywhere. Some are employed by large organizations to help in corporate planning, marketing and investment strategies, and financial planning. Some are hobbyists. Some have organizations devoted to planning for the future, including a Congressional Clearing House on the Future, firms to help clients plot their futures, academic centers for the study of the future, and activist groups to lobby Congress for futuristic considerations in legislative activity. Futurists have written numerous books, monographs, and articles about the future and futuristic research. They have become an integral part of our society; so it was to futurists that the committee turned for help.

WHO ARE THE FUTURISTS?

The World Future Society is the international association of futurists. During the last few years, its membership has nearly doubled and now totals 40,000 members. The society's activities include organizing conferences, establishing local chapters, and publishing a magazine, a journal, and an occasional book. Edward Cornish, who has been the president of the World Future Society for a number of years, has compiled a list of common characteristics of futurists. In his book, *The Study of the Future,* he writes that among futurists and their work is an openness to experience, a global outlook, a long-term perspective, an ecological orientation, a broad concern for humanity, rationality, pragmatism, reality of choice, an interest in values, optimism, and a sense of purpose. The committee, after talking with members of the World Future Society and other futurists, assembled its own list of traits common among futurists.

Futurists are liberals. They tend to ignore the study of the futures of institutions; they are more concerned with societies, cultures, and individuals. They are interested in international public policy—unregulated economic growth, technological advancement, and population expansion.

Futurists prefer change. The joy of being a futurist is to identify a change before it occurs. Futurists are more likely to focus on things that will change than on things that remain static.

Futurists are eclectic. They draw on various disciplines, including the natural and social sciences and the humanities, to facilitate their work.

Futurists emphasize changes in technology, the most obvious kind of change. Social, institutional, and other intangible changes are more elusive and therefore receive less attention from futurists.

Futurists are imaginative. Science fiction is a product of the discipline. Arthur C. Clarke and Isaac Asimov are both leading science fiction writers and leading futurists.

The committee believes that futurists are an invaluable asset to any organization or profession, such as local government, trying to look ahead. The futurists with whom members of the committee talked gave it clear directions for accomplishing the task of looking at local government in the year 2000.

FUTURISTIC THEORY AND METHODS

There are no facts about the future. Our predictions are at best no more than elegant speculations. Paul Dickson, in his book *The Future File*, describes some embarrassing predictions made by presumed experts in their respective fields:

"Whatever happens in Vietnam, I can conceive of nothing except military victory," said Dwight D. Eisenhower in 1967.

A *New York Times* editorial in 1903 called the prospect of manned flight a waste of time and money.

Following World War I a consulting firm told General Motors to eliminate its Chevrolet division because the car would never be successful.

These statements would not have been made by people who, like futurist Kenneth E. Boulding, believe in a "nonexistence theorem" about any prediction of the future of knowledge. "If we could predict it, we would know it now, we would have discovered it now, and we would not have to wait. All genuinely new information or knowledge has to be in some degree surprising; otherwise it is not new knowledge."

Three futures

Discovering the future is an exercise in manipulating time. There are futures, and there are futures of futures. The late John Osman, a nationally respected futurist and associate of the Brookings Institution, stated that there were really three futures: the next five years, the next eight to twelve years, and the distant future of twelve to twenty-five years hence. It is important to recognize the differences among the three and to know what changes are possible in each future.

Trends for the next five years generally are fixed and cannot be affected much by anything anyone wishes to do now. This future is fairly certain because very little will or can change.

Predictions for the next eight to twelve years are less accurate, but the opportunity to affect this future is greater. Some projects that are administered by local government, such as water and sewage systems, may be conceptualized and completed in this time.

Every vision of the future is a prism — altered by the values of the viewer.

David S. Arnold

Twelve to twenty-five years hence is a long time in which to plan and carry out important initiatives in the administration of local government. Despite social changes, it is a manageable span of time, one that encompasses some reassuring regularities as well as shocks.

Methods

Futurists use several imperfect methods to view the future, ranging from a look at history to the use of computer-based modeling.

As Boulding told the committee, the images of the past frequently are projected into the future—which is, perhaps, the great utility of history. It helps us learn more about the present and see the future more clearly.

Boulding also cautioned the committee. "History is biased against that which is durable—and there is no proposition that says the durable is the most important." In other words, writings and ruins endure time; but there is no assurance that they represent the truth, or what is most important. History also is very incomplete; the more distant it is the more incomplete it becomes. Barbara Tuchman's best-selling history of the fourteenth century, *A Distant Mirror*, is filled with speculation and interpretation of the durable record—a very incomplete one at that.

There are many rigorous *analytical tools* to propel us into the future. Mathematical or computer-based modeling is quite popular among some futurists. Jay Forrester's *Urban Dynamics* is essentially a model of the present and future in the form of equations and electronic data processing. Econometrics is a discipline that attempts to make economic predictions from computer-based models. Many securities analysts rely heavily on mathematical models to predict the future movements of given stocks or bonds.

Another popular quasi-analytical technique is the *delphi*. This method is a highly complex process of taking the views of presumed experts in a particular field and plumbing their minds for trends, values, and predictions about their special areas of competence. The method is designed by successively grouping and simplifying the views of the experts to produce a cogent statement about the probable futures in their field.

Then there are what might be called *intersubjective techniques*, which rely heavily on the human imagination to gather and analyze information about current trends and projections and apply them to the future. The technique is based on the belief that the "mind's eye" cited by Bronowski is a powerful tool for looking into the future. This technique was used by the committee in the last stages of its work.

To apply the intersubjective technique, however, an individual must journey into the future. Osman told the committee that the best management is done *from* the future; a person or a group emotionally, intellectually, perhaps even spiritually moves into the future, only to turn around and look back at the ground that has been covered.

Journeying into the future is a difficult trip. Most people resist it. It must be done in stages. The individual goes out, comes back, analyzes what was seen, and then goes out again. The trip can be seen in reverse sometimes when we suddenly find ourselves in a new and foreign culture or begin watching a movie that is set in some exotic locale. It takes time to adjust. In fact, Jack Finney has written a novel about the experiences of someone who goes back in time; it is called *Time and Again*. The subject is given the opportunity to visit Manhattan during the latter part of the nineteenth century. He finds the initial exposure overwhelming; he needs to return to the present, rest, and debrief himself. Then he goes back to the nineteenth century for a longer period of time, returns to the present, and rests. It takes a while for him to adjust fully to this emotional and intellectual journey.

The same is true of any imaginative trip into the future, especially for a large group of people trying together to apply an intersubjective technique.

The scenarios

The format that the committee chose for most of its work was the *scenario*. What is a scenario? Kenneth L. Kraemer has defined it as a description of events and conditions for studying an operating system. More specifically, he points out that scenarios are based on "projections of existing trends and predictions of future events, and also imaginings of what could be and might be." Kraemer then comments that scenarios work best for planning and developmental problems, to clarify major policy alternatives.

The scenario is a highly respected and frequently used technique for looking at the future. Ian Wilson, for one, has noted the value of alternative scenarios in trying to "bracket" the future. The committee began constructing simple scenarios about the future based on limited assumptions. "What would cars be like if there were no petroleum fuel?" "What would local government be like if there were no people under twenty years of age?"

The committee then graduated to building more elaborate alternative scenarios. Each part or member of the committee constructed a more complex scenario based on more explicit assumptions. "Assume you are an optimist, what would local government be like?" "Assume you are a pessimist . . . ?" And so on.

The purpose, as Wilson suggested, is to bracket the future. It is to get a clearer idea of the likely alternative futures that are twenty years away. The brackets to the future provide an opportunity to leave the present emotionally, to see the choices that are possible for the future, and to guide us in making the most desirable decisions now to achieve the chosen alternatives. Scenarios give us a better intellectual and intuitive feel for how present dynamics translate into future realities.

As the committee's deliberations progressed, five scenarios were developed for the year 2000: Careful Village, Hope County, Doubt Town, Delight Community, and Caution City (see Appendix B for full descriptions). Each scenario had parameters for energy, economy, society, demographics, values, communications, transportation, and other elements that impinge on local government. It was from the scenarios that the committee was able to arrive at the findings described later in this book.

The scenarios, in effect, are a knowledge base out of which the future can be fashioned. They are the means of intersubjectively applying that knowledge to the future.

THE FORCES OF CHANGE

Part 2 of this book covers forces of change that are largely external to local government and will affect it over the next twenty years. Although the committee dealt with dozens of indicators of change, only a few were sorted out to become the straws in the winds of change—the most significant indicators in today's world for changes in the future. These forces of change are grouped into five areas: economic forces, demographic shifts, urban patterns, technological changes, and politics.

Economic forces

Long-term economic prosperity is possible, but it will be preceded by a decade or more of difficult economic and social adjustments.

A sufficient supply of energy will be available in the year 2000 to support a prosperous economy—but it will not be cheap energy. The world's overwhelming reliance on petroleum will be reduced. Coal, the sun, synthetic fuels, and nuclear power will become more important. The development of these energy sources and the willingness to make optimum use of existing energy supplies are part of the economic adjustments of the next decade.

Scarcities of resources—including critical shortages of water, wood, precious metals, and clean air and water—will continue to plague communities throughout the next twenty years. These scarcities must be anticipated and adapted to throughout the period.

Inflation is eating away at the fabric of our economic system. Economists disagree on both the sources and the cures for inflation; however, all agree that the cures will be difficult, unpleasant, and slow to take effect. The public's "inflation psychology" needs to change; government spending must be curbed; productivity and innovation must be spurred; and capital investment must be encouraged.

Poverty will continue to be a national concern, but less so in the future than now. Encouraging steps have been taken in the past thirty years to reduce both the incidence and the severity of poverty, hunger, illiteracy, chronic unemployment, and environmental squalor. There is every reason to expect that the long-term prospect is for continued reduction—especially if the basic economic prediction of growth holds over the next twenty years. Even so, the paradox of poverty amidst affluence will not disappear. Society

will not be satisfied that it has done enough to reduce want and depriva-
tion—nor should it feel satisfied. Special assistance to the poor will still be
needed in 2000.

Demographic shifts

Current projections show important changes in the demographic profiles of
citizens of local governments in 2000.

How much change takes place in twenty years? Not as much as
you might think, especially in view of the popularity of Alvin
Toffler's **Future Shock.** Committee member Wayne Anderson
wondered aloud at the first meeting what would happen if we
suddenly were to go back twenty years in time. Say to 1960.
What would be different? What would be the same? The answer
is that there would be a lot of similarities: cars, TVs, airplanes,
elections, city halls, water treatment plants, PTAs, Boy Scouts,
Bob Hope, football, and miniature golf. The answer is that there
also would be a lot of differences: we would find more pollution
and crime perhaps; the civil rights movement would hardly
have been born; trust in all institutions would have been much
higher; color TV would have been a rarity at best. This kind of
speculation leaves a feeling that twenty years is not an
overwhelming span of time. It is really quite manageable in
terms of change. There may be some jolts, but there also are
some very reassuring regularities.

There will be more people we think of as elderly—over sixty-five years
of age. The median age of the population will increase over the next twenty
years, due to a stable or declining birth rate, increased longevity, and the
aging of the baby-boom generation.
   People will live in smaller households. Married couples will have fewer
children. People will probably continue to marry later in life. The rate of
divorce will increase, and fewer economic or social pressures for remar-
riage will exist.
   Women will continue to live longer than men, thus increasing their total
proportion of the population.
   Among minority groups, it is expected that the percentage of blacks in
the population will not change appreciably. By 1985 Hispanics will be the

largest single minority group in the United States and will continue to increase in size through 2000.

The pulls and tugs of these demographic changes will be felt everywhere. Competition for public resources between the elderly and the young will increase. Women will be increasingly important in economic life, and the social impact of their economic roles will be felt in the family, the community, and the nation. The smaller households, the trends favoring living alone, divorce, and women's greater independence augur weaker family ties and less community cohesiveness and stability.

Urban patterns

The shift to the Sunbelt will continue. Some demographers predict that such states as Florida, Arizona, and Nevada will show a 50 percent increase in population during the next ten years. It is expected that, as a result of the 1980 census, the Sunbelt may hold a majority of the seats in the U.S. House.

This shift to the Sunbelt could be affected by several factors, among them supplies of water and petroleum and availability of public services with the capacity to accommodate population increases. Residents in huge areas of the Sunbelt are even now living on a small supply of water. Mammoth public works projects will be needed to expand the supply to accommodate the anticipated growth. Further, these areas are highly dependent upon petroleum for transportation across the large areas of land between population centers, and, needless to say, petroleum supplies are not assured for the future.

Suburban sprawl will continue, but some changes are expected. Sprawl will not proceed at the post–World War II rate. It will tend to occur along travel corridors and around subregional commercial and industrial centers. The result will be what some have called "multinucleated metropolitan areas." Many exist today. They are areas in which the central city is no longer the single focus of work life, of major economic activity, of major sports and cultural events, of daily newspapers, radio, and TV. The trend toward decentralization of these functions is expected to continue.

Nonmetropolitan areas also may continue to grow, often at the apparent expense of metropolitan areas.

Technological changes

Telecommunications will bring about many changes, some currently unforeseen. Two-way information networks will make life much richer, although they probably will not be a cure-all for many basic problems that beset us.

Some people believe that by 2000, 100 million households will be connected by satellite, land-based cable, and other transmission systems.

Cable TV has a major interactive role to play in the future. People will be able to voice their opinions on both products and public policies from their homes—and they will see instantaneously how their views correspond with those of their neighbors.

In addition, the hookups will bring into the home a vast array of information, including entertainment, news, weather reports, school closings, traffic reports, transportation schedules, financial transactions, and local government service information. In some cases, people will be able to communicate directly with government agencies and counseling services using their cable systems and home keyboards.

These changes will be made possible through the widespread application of such technological innovations as microprocessors, fiber optics, and satellite relays.

Transportation technology, as a result of energy conservation, also will change in the coming years. Telecommunications occasionally will replace transportation. The automobile will remain the primary means of personal transportation, but it will be much more energy-efficient. Mass transit will become more economically viable as energy costs go up, although mass transit that requires vast amounts of capital investment, such as rapid rail, will be only a small part of the total transportation system.

Building technology also will improve, allowing for greater energy efficiency. "Smart" buildings will be common—buildings with major lighting, heating, cooling, and water systems centrally controlled by computers that are sensitive to changes in environmental conditions. New building materials will be available, as will new design features. All will require more flexible building codes.

Politics

Three major factors contribute to the feeling of powerlessness among local officials today. All can be expected to influence politics in the year 2000—but to a lesser extent.

The first factor is the pervasive intervention of the central (or federal) government in activities that once were solely the responsibility of the community and the local government. The result has been that as much as one-half of some local governments' budgets are provided and controlled directly by the central government. Thus, few local decisions or initiatives may be undertaken without close attention to central government regulations, dictates, policies, and opinions—which frequently are inconsistent and conflicting.

Second, the courts have become the final appeal on thousands of decisions that once were thought to be entirely legislative. These decisions frequently go beyond prevailing national concerns such as civil rights.

Finally, a factor in the feeling of powerlessness is the whipsaw of public opinion, caused by powerful but contradictory forces. One dimension of the whipsaw is the feeling by the public that the citizens pay too much in taxes and that the government spends too much. Hence the tax revolts that have become so popular. At the same time, governments are besieged with requests from special groups for greater services. Sometimes citizens are tax revolutionaries and special group members simultaneously.

Another dimension of the whipsaw is the popular desire to hold public officials accountable for their actions while withholding their power to act—a desire that confers responsibility without authority.

Both dimensions are, in part, results of Watergate and the era of bad feeling that followed the war in Vietnam—both understandably divisive events. The whipsaw also may be an expression of frustration about inflation, slowed economic growth, and the accumulated effects of income redistributions. Local elected and appointed officials, in other words, may simply be scapegoats, a possibility that understandably increases their feeling of powerlessness.

There is every prospect that the factors contributing to this powerlessness will be with us in the year 2000, but the committee believes they can all be reduced in intensity. Thus, the feeling of powerlessness will abate.

NURTURING THE ESSENTIAL COMMUNITY

Part 3 of this book identifies local government strategies for contending with the major forces of change in society over the next twenty years.

The theme that guides Part 3 is the idea that the way to maintain a strong and independent local government is through nurturing the *essential community*. As the committee looked into the future, it was convinced that local governments must not lose sight of their mission to provide services that enhance or preserve the essential nature of their communities. These are not just basic services; they go beyond police, fire, and sanitation. Yet they are well within the control of local government. They are the services that deal with the quality of neighborhoods, homes, schools, streets, and commercial and industrial areas. They are what local governments manage best; they are the essence of the community.

The committee foresees a number of essential *strategies* for local governments over the next twenty years as they seek to maintain strength and independence while nurturing their essential communities. These strategies are not based on simplistic assumptions of growth.

One strategy is to *learn to get by modestly*. The era of massive growth in the public sector has ended. In the foreseeable future all levels of government will have to adapt to limited growth in tax revenue and other resources.

The era of modest growth means changes in the ways local governments operate. Budgets should not be fashioned with a margin for incremental growth in expenditures. There must be more cooperation between the public and private sectors. Strong alliances with the scientific and academic communities are required. A greater emphasis needs to be placed on volunteerism. Citizens should be assisted in doing for themselves what they now expect local governments to do. Public policies designed to reduce risks to zero will need reexamination. Efforts should be made to make local government employment more satisfying, and a major agenda item for the future should be the maintenance of the local infrastructure.

Another strategy for local governments in the future should be to *regulate the demand for government services and public goods*. Pricing mechanisms are the key. Imposing a price on a good or service establishes a threshold of demand. The amount charged need not be the full price, but it should be high enough so that the service is used primarily by those who truly need it.

At the same time local governments can do their part to reduce economic demand in general. Policies may be adopted to encourage energy conservation, for example.

Local governments need a third strategy for coping with the future—*exercise greater skepticism about the value of central (or federal) government grants and transfers*. In some cases, this means choosing to buy back a portion of a city's, county's, or COG's independence from the central government. It may mean doing without some nonessential, but admittedly desirable, programs. It also can mean exchanging central government money for local funds.

These are risky actions, but necessary ones if local government is to remain relatively independent, and if local officials are to regain more of their ability to affect the nature of their communities.

A fourth strategy for the future should be to *reevaluate the scale of local government*. Traditionally, to regionalize has been to reform; today this is not necessarily the case.

Government that is decentralized to the level of communities and neighborhoods may be the wave of the future. A reduction in the scale of decision making and service delivery may be the only way to build citizen support for local government—and it may prove to be the most effective way of delivering many services.

The fifth strategy for local governments will be to *alter the mix of services* performed to adapt to coming demographic shifts.

Services must adjust as the population ages, as women become a more important economic and political force, and as minorities remain important segments of the community. Service delivery must recognize the growth of the Hispanic minority, the decline in the size of households, and the decreased role of the nuclear family.

The profession

Finally, the committee took a look at its own image in the year 2000. What do these major forces of change and recommended strategies mean for the profession of appointed managers in local government?

They mean a lot. They mean that this will be a much more *heterogeneous* profession in the future—with many more minority members, women, and administrators serving not only in cities, but also in many more counties, COGs, and even some special service districts.

They mean that the profession will experience the very same whipsaw experienced by elected officials. Professional administrators, like elected officials, will find themselves seeking *far greater security*. Employment agreements, executive search organizations, third-party intervention—these are all waves of the future.

They mean that managing will involve *brokering, negotiating, coordinating*. They mean less reliance on analytical and supervisory skills, less reliance on the legal basis of the professional management position, and much more emphasis on the interpersonal skills of the incumbent.

The changes and strategies will mean a profession that becomes even more important to the successful operation of local governments, a profession that will—by the very challenge of its task and the importance of the outcomes—attract the best administrative talent in the country. They mean people able to understand and respond to the major forces acting on local governments and to help elected officials carry out the many strategies necessary to nurture the essential community.

Part 2

A national settlement system

The forces of change

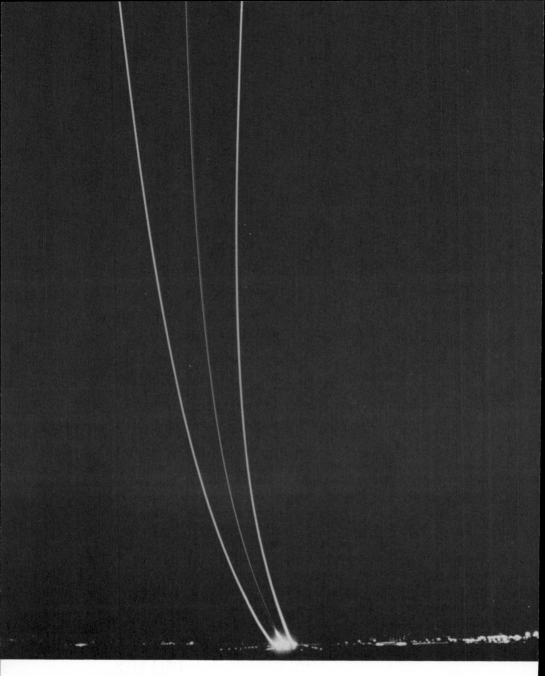

All great changes are irksome to the human mind, especially
those which are attended with great dangers and uncertain
effects.

John Adams

A national settlement system

What is "urban" is by no means clear, and continuing use of outmoded meanings deflects the policy debate at the outset. There is good reason to argue that regional patterns have so changed that the notion that some things are "urban" and some things are not no longer has theoretical significance, analytic utility, or policy relevance in a national society with a national settlement system.

A national society is an interdependent society in which increasingly effective communications provide speedier and more potent feedback than ever before. Interdependence guarantees that the consequences of new policy initiatives will—for good or ill—and all too frequently counterintuitively, quickly reverberate throughout the settlement system as a whole.

The classic regional organization of the national economy was one of the northeastern industrial belt, localized during the first three quarters of the nineteenth century between the capital stocks and entrepreneurial skills of the east coast metropolitan centers and the coal and iron resources of the midwest, linked to a constellation of resource-dependent hinterland regions by rail and water transportation routes radiating from gateway cities and growing as a result of a process of circular and cumulative causation.

Today, this classic regionalization no longer exists. The glue of centrality that restricted innovative new developments to the core cities of the industrial heartland has been dissolved. Regions throughout the nation are sharing in the newer forms of industrial and post-industrial employment growth. New highways, integrated road-rail systems (piggyback) and land-sea systems (containerization), jet aircraft and air freight, and new forms of communication have virtually eliminated the classic localizing effects of transport inputs and the significance of proximity in speedy transmission of new ideas and practices. The economy's rapid growth industries (electronics, aerospace, scientific instruments, etc.) are dispersed throughout the former exurban, non-metropolitan, and sunbelt peripheries, and they are being followed by the postindustrial management and control functions of the private sector.

There now are growing groups of *national* citizens whose ties are to peer groups sharing common job experiences and life styles located in particular kinds of communities within every region of the nation. Interests are shared in common across these communities and, linked by the interchange of migration, such life style communities are closer to each other in perception and attitudes than they are to geographically-contiguous neighborhoods offering alternative life styles to different population sub-groups. Each region in the nation now offers a common and increasing array of life style communities so that on the one hand inter-regional differentiation has diminished while on the other intra-regional segmentation has increased. In establishing the life-style array, there is also an increasing appreciation and use of each region's particular array of amenities although assessed relative to the amenities of other regions, as well as a sharper discounting of their disadvantages, including negative externalities. In short, there is now a national system of settlement.

The increase in the array of life styles comes from opposing but interrelated trends. National interdependence, increasingly tightly woven by more potent forms of communication, has brought with it countervailing tendencies for particular sub-cultures to assert their independent identity or for new sub-cultures to try to invent one.

The lesson that the new communications media could be instrumental in the process of social activation was first learned in civil rights, and most effectively exploited by the environmentalists. The result is that there is now increasing pluralism based upon various forms of sub-cultural intensification: racial, ethnic, life cycle (swingles, gentrifiers, the elderly "snow-birds," etc.), and based upon a range of other types of preferences (hippie, homosexual, etc).

Yet this intensification has only been possible because of the relativity afforded by nationwide communications: each group can exist because it can establish its separate identity not only by an internal process, but also through comparative perceptions created via the communications media. And because of the potency and immediacy of the medium, there is a nationwide imagery that transcends locality, and a speed and commonality of subgroup response that negates older leads and lags of metropolis-centered dependency. No longer does a new idea, fashion, or fad appear in the big city and play itself out twenty years later in the rural periphery. Time-space convergence has produced a differentiated but highly intercon- nected national society and economy.

The fact that we now must deal with a national time-space demands that we replace our older urban theory, approach our analysis in different ways, and rethink our approaches to policy. The category "urban" is without utility. We err if we do not talk about a national settlement system with developmental initiatives and feedbacks that reverberate in a national time- space. To understand the dynamics of any particular locality such as a legal central city, we must know its relative position within the pathways of change that extend from today's developmental frontiers not those of yesterday, however nostalgic we may feel.

There is no reason to believe that aging industrial cities will be able to revitalize unless they are able to develop a new high technology activity base. Neither is there any reason to believe that those metropolitan regions developing such a base will do so in a manner which recreates the inner cities of the past. Unless there is a prolonged recession, there is little basis for believing that private market revitalization of inner city neighborhoods will diffuse much further, and if recession is a necessary condition, emergence from recession—surely a more significant goal—would equally surely curtail it. There is every reason therefore to believe that settlement patterns that have emerged in the past decade will continue to diffuse and differentiate.

The form of the future growth of the nation's settlement system will depend ultimately on the form of new employment growth. The leading edge has always been that delivered by effective research and development, and much of the recent pattern of change has been an expression of the innova- tion and extension of new forms of post-industrial activity. Communications and the computer appear to be the key, and the reduction of national access differences has led to preferences for amenity-rich small town sunbelt loca- tions, preferences which are consistent with energy and environment choice. The two critical questions are whether technological leadership can be maintained, and whether employment opportunities will exist for the disadvantaged.

Although their populations are decreasing, older central cities will hold a very large number of people whose lives and fortunes are unfavorably affected by their physical and social environment. There is and will be a continuing problem of ameliorating the heavy social costs incurred by the concentration of captive individuals without access to the real economy, concentrations which continue to be characterized by high unemployment rates, especially among minorities, and by low educational achievement, drug addiction, crime, and a sense of hopelessness and alienation from society. Attention to causes rather than symptoms demands that factors which exclude individuals from the mainstream of society and from meaningful work opportunities be of prime concern, for work is a measure of worth in the U.S.

Source: Excerpted from Brian J. L. Berry, "Urban Futures: Another View," paper written for the National Urban Policy Roundtable held in Washington, D.C., February 7, 1980. The roundtable, a project of the Charles F. Kettering Foundation, is coordinated by the Academy for Contemporary Problems.

The forces of change

Local government in the year 2000 will be affected by many forces, some of which can be anticipated now. Among the agents of change examined by the committee were economic forces, demographic shifts, urban patterns, technological changes, and politics.

ECONOMIC FORCES

"Over the last 100 years," Kenneth E. Boulding told the committee late one evening, "we have been incredibly lucky." He was speaking about the growth of the economy. He went on to say that, with the discovery of the energy potential of oil and natural gas, it was as if we had found a "huge treasure chest in the basement. And what do you do when you discover the treasure chest in the basement? You all know the answer to that. You live it up."

Living it up is what the North American economy has been doing for the last hundred years; it has been spending its treasure as if it were an unlimited resource. The economy has been fueled by the discovery of abundant and inexpensive energy.

Before 1970, according to a report by the Council of State Governments (CSG), the price per unit of electricity had declined for more than seventy years. "The more we used," observed committee member Norman King, "the cheaper the unit price."

Our luck may be running out. We may have reached a point at which the downward slope of the curve has ended. "Between 1970 and 1975," notes CSG, "the price of electricity increased by 60 percent." New electrical units cost more than existing ones, an example of classic inflation. It will cost more to use more of the same.

Our luck with the energy supply is only one factor in producing our current wealth—thus only one factor considered by the committee in its evaluation of the economic environment for local governments in the future. Many other factors also helped boost our economy—technological innovation, skilled and productive labor, availability of investment capital, consensus on economic goals, political stability, favorable international trade balances, and abundant natural resources. Every economist may have a different list, but each is a long list—and energy is only one item on it.

The committee's task was to sort through the future of these and other factors, examine them, and see what they promised for North American wealth between now and 2000.

The committee reached the following conclusions:

The next ten years will bring difficult, though not debilitating, economic adjustments.

The greatest adjustment will be to learn to live with more expensive energy.

The economy can grow at a prudent rate over the next twenty years—although not as rapidly as it has grown during the last thirty years—provided some tough decisions are made.

The growth of the public sector of the economy probably will continue, but at a slower rate.

The committee anticipates that the country must make adjustments and overcome obstacles, but these changes are within the range of possibility. Americans will be adjusting to a new balance between available resources and life styles. The ability to control inflation, to improve productivity, to increase capital investment, and to adapt to the cost and type of energy we use are a few of those adjustments.

Energy

Every futurist agrees that energy is the single most important consideration affecting the economic horizon. Will there be enough? What kind will it be? Is it affordable?

Each one answers the questions differently, but the committee believes there is a theme throughout most of the analyses. Energy will be more expensive, but it will be available in quantities large enough to fuel a healthy economy—provided the right political, social, and economic decisions are made now.

There is a huge amount of information about energy that can be used to project the future. "But evidence is not the same thing as truth," warned Boulding. Evidence is abundant, but the truth is scarce indeed. Evidence is contradictory and suspect. It is almost always a by-product of the debate over whether or not further economic growth is desirable.

People who view growth as desirable tend to foresee enough energy to sustain current levels of growth and industrial development. People who are alarmed about the environmental, social, and political consequences of growth foresee an energy shortage.

The truth, as opposed to the evidence, is probably where it usually can be found—somewhere in the middle. In other words, one group sees the glass half empty; the other group sees it half full. They do not disagree so much about the facts; they do, however, interpret the facts differently.

Frequently the greatest difference between groups is the degree of optimism or pessimism they have about the ability of Americans to make adjustments to changes in the nature and cost of energy. Denis Hayes illustrates the problem. "We are *not* running out of energy," he argues. "However, we *are* running out of cheap oil and gas." The energy sources are there; but they will be costly.

Hayes's social, economic, and political interpretation is that "we are running out of money to pay for doubling and redoubling an already vast energy supply system. We are running out of political willingness to accept the social costs of continued rapid energy expansion. We are running out of the environmental capacity needed to handle the waste generated in energy production. And we are running out of time to adjust to these new realities."

OIL AND GAS   By far the most important source of energy currently is petroleum. The Edison Electric Institute reports that in 1975 more than 75 percent of the energy in the United States came from oil and natural gas. In 1950 the figure was approximately 40 percent.

"We're hooked on it," observed Dr. Joel Snow of the U.S. Department of Energy (DOE) while appearing before the committee, "and overall prospects for finding more petroleum in the future are not great." Almost every prediction about the availability of gas and oil shows that production will decrease by the year 2000. Supplies of petroleum will be less than demand.

A study sponsored by the Massachusetts Institute of Technology predicts a growth in oil production for approximately fifteen years—assuming there are no production restrictions such as those that might be imposed by the national government or the OPEC cartel to stretch existing supplies. But it could be worse; production could level off as early as 1985 so that by 2000, the cost of oil could be dramatically higher than it is today.

ALTERNATIVE SOURCES   The prospects for an easy and inexpensive conversion to a nonpetroleum-based economy appear dim. There will be no quick fixes, Snow told the committee: "Technology may not save us." Technologists may hold out the promise, he said, but they are "incurable optimists."

There are other sources of energy for large-scale industrial, residential, and transportational use. There are also possibilities for conservation of petroleum energy. The technology for these alternatives exists or could be developed soon, but it will be costly.

Coal is a possible substitute for petroleum, especially in the production of electricity. Some projections indicate that the United States might have enough coal to meet the country's energy needs indefinitely. One estimate shows that the United States has 435 billion tons of recoverable coal, a resource greater than all the oil in the Middle East. Extraction of the coal, however, poses serious environmental problems, The attempts being made to convert coal into natural gas, as noted by Dr. Kenneth Friedman of DOE, face some technological barriers and are very expensive.

In addition to the coal, there are perhaps 700 billion barrels of extractable oil in shale rock formations within the United States—but, again, there are environmental drawbacks to extraction.

Nothing endures but change.

Heraclitus

Nuclear power might be another viable source of energy. But the accident at the Three Mile Island reactor in Pennsylvania, significant political opposition, and the need for huge capital investments make its availability as a major substitute for petroleum by the year 2000 very tenuous.

Solar energy remains a possibility—but only for small-scale use. It is unlikely that it will be of value to large-scale industries.

Richard Rowberg of the congressional Office of Technology Assessment told the committee that solar energy could be very useful for residential and some commercial uses. No new technology is needed; there are no apparent economies of scale; and there are no technological barriers to integrating solar energy with electrical power. Solar energy has the potential to become a major source of power for residential heating and cooling systems and for use on conglomerations of homes and office buildings.

In today's market solar energy is not yet economically feasible; it costs more than conventional energy. But when oil becomes more expensive, significant trade-offs will occur. The intermediate step is to make certain that buildings erected today and in the future can be retrofitted for solar use.

Progress from unexpected sources should not be overlooked. The newsletter *Footnotes to the Future,* for instance, reports that DOE foresees considerable potential in hydroelectric power from small dams. The newsletter quotes a United Nations organization as saying that hydroelectric power might yield more energy than nuclear, solar, or wind sources by the year 2000.

CONSERVATION   Some have argued that even more important than the development of new energy sources is the conservation of existing sources. A major study issued in 1979 by a team of scholars from the Harvard Business School states that "the prospect for dramatic *increases* in domestic supplies from the four conventional fuels—oil, gas, coal, and nuclear—is bleak." This six-year study concluded that efforts to encourage conservation and solar energy rather than total reliance on conventional sources "make good economic sense."

The study proposes a large-scale program of energy conservation in addition to efforts to increase domestic fuel supplies.

The committee explored some of the avenues of conservation—petroleum conservation, for instance. Dr. Kennerly Digges of the U.S. Department of Transportation (DOT) told the committee that one-third of the petroleum used in the United States is for automobiles. Significant economies can be realized in this area—they already have been. If the government succeeds in enforcing its fuel economy standards for U.S. auto manufacturers, the average miles per gallon will increase from 19 in 1979 to 27.5 in 1985.

Mass transit will help conservation efforts, but transportation specialist Henry Nejako of DOT says that it will not make much difference between now and 1985. Today mass transit accounts for only 5 percent of the total transportation system. Thus it will not make a significant dent in the petroleum problem before 2000.

COST   Alternatives are available to replace petroleum energy, to stretch the supply of petroleum, and to increase the time needed for further technological breakthroughs.

People need to move toward these alternatives fairly soon. Incentives that might facilitate the necessary shifts include government regulation, artificial reduction of supplies to decrease consumption, and taxes and other measures to increase cost. People might voluntarily make the move by installing the apparatus for conversion to solar energy and by making more use of mass transit.

The committee believes that the market system will eventually cause the shift—provided that energy subsidies are reduced. When the cost of transportation or heating or cooling becomes a large enough percentage of disposable income, people will search for less expensive sources or at least for those that are no more expensive. Thus, petroleum will be displaced once it is comparable in cost to other energy sources. It is difficult to judge when that may occur, but the sooner people begin to make changes, for whatever reason, the more likely it is that there will be a sufficient energy supply.

The conclusion of the committee is that the energy is available for continued economic growth, but it will be more expensive. Difficult decisions have to be made—decisions that are by and large out of the hands of local governments. James O'Toole and colleagues at the University of Southern California's Center for Futures Research take a similar position. They foresee the possibility of a quality economy in the long run—an economy with reduced waste, inefficiency, and pollution; with more satisfying and plentiful jobs; and with more goods that contribute to a high quality of life. "Whether the nation achieves this quality economy or inherits an economy of scarcity hinges on how effectively decision makers in the public and private sectors make substitutions for scarce forms of energy."

Decisions need to be made about the risks and costs of nuclear energy, the amount of money available to avoid or repair damage to the environment, and the degree to which present economic growth can be deferred in order to conserve petroleum and develop alternative sources more fully.

The work force

The relative size and composition of the work force in the United States will require some economic adjustments also. The facts turn on some demographic projections that will be discussed later, but the projections are summarized here.

Demographers, noting the declining birth rate, predict that the growth in the size of the work force will level off over the next twenty years. Some find this alarming; others do not. The committee shares the alarm but sees ways in which growth in the labor market can be accommodated.

Ian Wilson states that the size of the labor force is a key to economic growth and that there will be a slowdown in the growth of the force. "Overall,

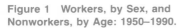

Figure 1 Workers, by Sex, and Nonworkers, by Age: 1950–1990.

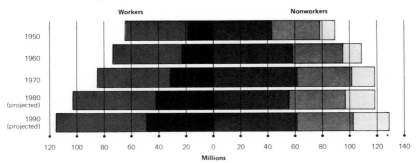

Note: Workers as defined here are those persons 16 years of age and over in the civilian labor force or the armed forces; nonworkers are those persons under 16 years of age and persons 16 and over who are not in the labor force. The sustained rise in the size of the United States labor force is largely a result of the corresponding rise in the size of the working age population. The prospective changes in the age composition of the population and the labor force imply a substantial decline in the ratio of nonworkers to workers. Further de-

cline is expected by 1985 and 1990 assuming that the fertility rate remains at or near the replacement level implied by the Series II projections described in Figure 3.

labor force growth will do well to average 1.1 percent per year," he writes, compared with the average of 1.6 percent since 1950.

This knowledge, however, does not concern many economists. The decline in births is being offset by increased immigration, delayed retirement, and the continued entry of women into the work force. *Business Week* cites economist Larry Neal of the University of Illinois: "With zero population growth, productivity would tend to increase as the result of greater investment in physical and human capital, and we might even improve the rate of advance of technological progress."

Public sector

The size of the public sector is one of the key decisions that Americans will be making over the next twenty years. The outcome of this decision, which is a current battle being fought in many different arenas, will be a major economic adjustment with significant consequences for local government. Even so, the committee expects the public sector to grow at a slower rate over the next twenty years than it has grown during the last thirty.

The public sector of the U.S. economy—and the intervention by regulation and preemption of the government into private economic activity—began during the Depression. During the 1930s, government expenditures were about 10 percent of the gross national product (GNP); in 1973 they were 32 percent. The federal government has intervened to regulate major portions of the private sector, as well as activities common to most private businesses.

The outcome of long-range efforts to curb inflation and promote growth may depend on decisions about the size of the public sector. Some people who once uncritically favored the growth of this sector now wonder whether restraining its growth is the only hope of fighting inflation and promoting general economic health.

In 1979 the report of the Joint Economic Committee of Congress, adopted unanimously for the first time in twenty years, stated that stagflation may be the result of growing federal programs. The only cure for the condition is to restrain demand by cutting government expenditures and to stimulate supply by cutting taxes and regulations. The correlation between the size of government and inflation is evident, according to U.S. Comptroller General Elmer Staats. Over one-half of the federal budget is indexed to the cost of living, thus promoting a vicious economic circle.

Boulding cited the low productivity of the U.S. economy as one of the causes for the growth of the government's portion of GNP. He and several others considered the probability of a productivity growth rate of zero—or even less.

Will and Intellect are one and the same thing.

Benedict (Baruch) Spinoza

The taxpayer revolt of the late 1970s also concerns the size of the public sector. On one level the revolt is properly interpreted as citizens' frustrations with rising taxes and unsatisfactory services from all levels of government. It is their attempt—though often misguided—to impose discipline on a government that they perceive as inefficient.

But many have argued that the revolt encompasses broader issues—that it is an attempt to limit the size of the public sector by checking the future growth of education, welfare, health, and other social service programs. Some of those programs are national health insurance, national income maintenance, imposition of national standards for retirement programs, and the regulation of various industries. All these issues will take from five to ten years to resolve nationally, and their possible resolutions are by no means clear.

The trends of public sector growth during the last forty years will not change easily. This seems especially true in light of the fact that the public sector is even larger in many European and Asian countries that are our economic competitors. The current taxpayer revolt and the resolution of the difficulties with programs such as national health insurance indicate a desire to decrease the growth rate of the public sector. Thus the committee predicts that over the years this sector and the role of local government in the economy will grow—although at a significantly slower rate.

Obstacles

The committee is confident that the U.S. economy can adjust to changes in the nature and cost of energy, the size of the labor market, and the resolution of the debate over the size of the public sector. It is less confident that a number of obstacles facing continued healthy growth can be overcome. These, more than energy and other adjustments, will determine our economic horizons.

The obstacles include inflation, productivity, and technological innovation. The prospect of continued high inflation, decreased productivity in the private and public sectors, and the disturbingly low level of technological innovation in recent years in the United States are alarming indicators for our economic future.

INFLATION   It is hard to overdramatize the problems caused by inflation or the difficulties of curbing it in the years ahead. As the United States enters the 1980s, it is experiencing the worst inflation in its history. Surprisingly, inflation has not played a major role in U.S. economic history. Gabriel Hauge has conducted research showing that in 1945 wholesale prices were no higher than they were in 1875. Since 1966, however, the consumer price index, which reflects inflation and other factors, has increased at an average annual rate of 6 percent, compared to a rate of 1.7 percent from 1948 through 1965.

This inflation is pernicious in its cumulative effects. It makes economic or financial planning difficult; it frustrates attempts to save money; it distorts market forces; and it leads to despair. Amitai Etzioni, a sociologist with Columbia University, was quoted in the *Wall Street Journal* as saying, "Inflation is threatening the psychological safety of people. They can't retire or save to put their kids through school. All bets are off."

The effects of inflation on local governments are similar, making it increasingly difficult to project annual revenues and expenditures or to plan for long-range financial needs. Inflation increases real estate values, thus leading citizens to organize tax revolts.

The committee discovered an increased understanding of the nature of this inflation. Although such an understanding does not lead to specific and politically viable solutions, it does suggest the harshness of the economic adjustments to be made. The *Wall Street Journal,* after conducting a major study and talking to the nation's leading economists, states that "inflation is the inevitable result of the kind of economy and society that we have been shaping for decades, a society in which both individuals and businesses are protected against the worst economic hazards of earlier eras and consumption is favored over savings and investment."

Among those interviewed by the *Journal* was Robert Solow, a leading liberal economist, who believes that "the single most important reason for inflation is that we are a society that has tried to prevent deep recessions, to provide income security for people and to help those who suffer." Inflation, he believes, is the price we pay for "becoming a more-humane society." Many more conservative economists agree.

Inflation also causes a change in people's behavior. Years of unremitting inflation have conditioned people to expect more inflation, and they have developed an inflationary psychology. They do not save; they buy now because they believe prices will increase. They push for wages that are indexed to inflation. Businesses set wages and prices with a margin for inflation. Prices, for instance, no longer fall during recessions as they did in the past because businesses know that the government will spend us out of a recession quickly enough for them to sell the goods at a high price.

Contributing to this inflation is the cost of government regulation. Environmental controls, occupational health and safety standards, price supports, and market regulation all contribute to the cost of regulation. The cost of farm price supports, beef and steel import restrictions, a higher minimum wage, and increased social security taxes equaled about one-third of the inflation in 1978.

The need to curb inflation is clear, but the difficulties implicit in the foregoing statements are impressive and suggest some of the economic adjustments necessary during the 1980s.

PRODUCTIVITY   Another economic problem faced by the U.S. economy has been an alarming drop in productivity. The severity of the problem is in some dispute. Noting that "productivity is the average output for every hour of labor, and it's been declining steadily for the past 15 years or so," the *Washington Post* regarded the news editorially as "somber."

Some economists believe that there was no reason for alarm during the first half of that period. Until about 1974, argues Edward F. Denison of the Brookings Institution's Economic Studies program, much of that decline was due to a decrease in the number of people moving from farm to nonfarm jobs, an increase in the proportion of younger people and a consequent decrease of skilled workers in the labor force, and regulations by Congress. By 1974, however, productivity had fallen at an alarming rate. It declined by nearly 5 percent that year and by 0.7 percent the next year. Although it increased in the following years, the increases were very small.

The result of the decline in productivity, writes Denison, is "a strongly adverse impact on living standards, business costs, inflation, and government revenues. The dip also has intensified the stagflation dilemma." Denison is not sure he can explain the low productivity. Two possibilities are the decline in research and development (R&D) and the cost of government regulation. Another is the shift from an economy dominated by agriculture and manufacturing to one dominated by services and government. These sectors are less susceptible to increases in productivity.

The next decade is the time when the decline in productivity must be better understood—and turned around. Without better economic productivity in the 1980s, a healthy economy in the 1990s will be wishful thinking.

INNOVATION   Many believe that the decline in R&D in the United States in recent years has led to a decline in innovations that translate into productivity and competitiveness in world markets.

Half the patents issued in the United States in 1978, according to John Heimann, U.S. Comptroller of the Currency, were issued to foreigners. In 1960, the U.S. Department of Commerce reports, foreigners were issued only about one-fifth of the patents. Stanford Research Institute found that in the 1950s, 82 percent of the major inventions brought to market were produced in the United States. By the late 1960s, the United States accounted for only 55 percent of the total.

The cause of the decline of innovation is generally believed to be the decline of research and development. According to the National Science Foundation, federal investment in R&D has declined 5 percent since 1960, and its percentage of GNP has declined also.

The notion of spending more on R&D comes at a time when most believe that federal expenditures generally are too high, and efforts are being made to balance the federal budget. In addition, inflation has increased the cost of R&D dramatically, and federal regulation appears hostile to private research and development.

The outlook

If the United States economy is to make the necessary adjustments, it will need to develop new energy sources, conserve existing sources, pay more for energy, limit inflation, increase productivity, and spur technological development. Yet the committee does not find the adjustments improbable nor the obstacles insurmountable. There can be sufficient energy supplies. The labor force can be adequate and promote growth. The debate on the size of the public sector can be resolved. And inflation need not be chronic; increases in productivity need not be small; and neither investment nor research and development need be impoverished.

The committee believes that the necessary adjustments will be made in the next ten years, and individuals and their local governments will prosper in an economy that will be growing prudently.

Poverty will be reduced as the proportion of the population unable to take care of its basic needs shrinks. Encouraging steps have been taken in the past thirty years to reduce both the incidence and the severity of poverty, hunger, illiteracy, chronic unemployment, and squalor. There is every reason to expect that the long-term prospect is for continued reduction—particularly if the basic economic outlook for prudent growth holds over the next twenty years—but the paradox of poverty amidst affluence will not disappear entirely.

The committee's optimism may not be as great as that of Buckminster Fuller, who believes that "it is highly feasible within ten years to have all humanity living at a higher standard of living than anyone knows." It is reasonable, however, to infer that in a prudently growing economy, the standard of living will improve. Consumption will not be as conspicuous as it has been. People will be better able to satisfy their needs, indulge in some of their desires, improve their communities, and, overall, enjoy a better quality of life.

DEMOGRAPHIC SHIFTS

In search of the straws in the wind that blow toward the future of American local government, the committee looked closely for clues about people. Who will be the citizens of our cities and counties in twenty years? What will be the composition of the population?

The search revealed some curious facts about the United States—facts that invite a search for explanations. The committee found that:

The fashion model currently in greatest demand is over thirty years old.

Family size has decreased by 10 percent in the last fourteen years.

The sports editor of the *New York Times* is a woman.

Fifty percent of the kindergarten students in Los Angeles are Hispanic.

The committee found that these curiosities are in fact harbingers of the future. They signal some profound changes in the composition of American society between now and 2000.

Demography is destiny.

Laurence Rutter

To understand these curiosities, the committee turned to the work of demographers. Demographers are producing a tremendous amount of data about the composition of American society and a vast array of sophisticated projections about where past and current trends will take us in the future. The data will surely increase with the full analysis of the 1980 census.

The committee found a gold mine of information in *Social Indicators, 1976*, issued by the U.S. Bureau of the Census in 1977. The volume is a massive compilation of trends in the U.S. population, including projections to the year 2000 and in some cases beyond. What makes the data even more forceful is the near unanimity among experts about what to expect in the future.

There is, however, one caveat about demography that was issued by Kenneth Boulding. He noted that the available population projection data are practically celestial in their regularity. In the absence of unforeseen trends, it is very easy to project these data into the future. It is those unforeseen trends that always upset demographers' projections. Thus, the unexpected can make most of the data useless.

In any case, the committee foresees a citizenry that is much older than today's population, that has a greater proportion of females, that is more likely to be isolated from family units, and that is likely to have a greater number of Spanish-speaking members than blacks.

Age

The population is aging. Emphasis is no longer on the young but is shifting to the middle-aged and the elderly. This shift is reflected in a number of ways, some of which are:

The median age today is twenty-nine; in the year 2010 it will be thirty-five.

In 1940, 34 percent of the population was nineteen years of age or under. In 1970, the ratio had jumped to 38 percent, but by the year 2000, that group will total only 30 percent of the population.

In 1940, only 7 percent of the population was sixty-five and over. In 1970, the figure was 10 percent, and in the year 2000 it is expected to be 12 percent.

There will be 10 million more people sixty-five and over in the year 2000 than in 1970.

Several forces are at work behind these shifts. The first is the aging of what demographers have called the baby-boom cohort group. The second is the steady decline in the fertility rate.

Everyone who was born during the great surge in births following World War II is in his or her twenties or thirties today. By the year 2000, they will be in their forties and fifties. People belonging to this group include those who in the mid-1960s exhorted others never to trust anyone over thirty. As this group passes through the generations, it will show as a bulge in the population charts.

Fertility for the past several years has been at or even below the population replacement rate, which is an average of 2.1 births for every woman. Among the factors contributing to the low birth rate are the availability of contraceptive devices, the legality of abortion, late marriages, a greater frequency of divorces, and an increase in the number of women in the work force.

These forces probably will continue for the next twenty years. Contraception will still be available, and abortion will remain as an option (although organized opposition may succeed in discouraging its marginal use). There is no reason to believe that society will discourage late marriages and frequent divorces; and there is every indication that women will play an even greater role in the work force.

The prospect for continued aging of the U.S. population was one of the committee's most fascinating demographic findings. Even more striking is

**Figure 2 Population Under 25 Years
of Age, by Selected Age Groups:
1940–2000.**

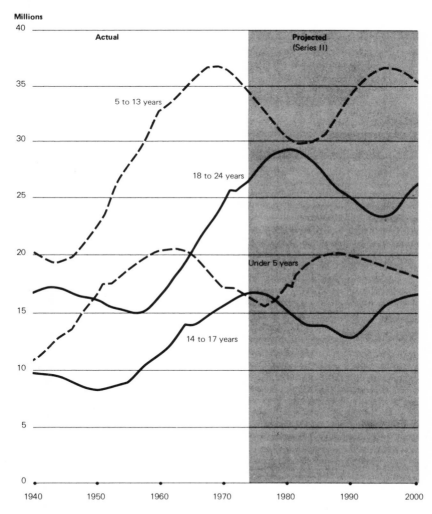

Note: The actual and projected populations of persons under 25 are shown in this figure. The specific age groups were selected to provide school administrators as well as lawmakers with basic information on the general size of each population group and the interrelationships of the past, present, and future school population. These data are based on the Series II population projections described in Figure 3.

the speed at which this phenomenon is occurring. Reporter James C. Hyatt writes in the *Wall Street Journal* that "recent gains have already upset some projections: In 1975, the number of people aged 65 and older was 4.1% higher than had been expected five years earlier."

This aging of the population is one of the most frequent bases on which speculation about the future is built, and futurists generally are concerned about the economic, social, and political consequences of this change in the composition of the population.

Hyatt foresees a possible 75 percent increase in nursing home residents from 1975 to 1990, a projection that has prompted others to look at the whole question of nursing homes. Fred Dudden, director of the information service at the Davis Institute for the Care and Study of Aging in Denver, says that between 20 and 50 percent of nursing home residents need not be there. He believes many older people will return to cities from outlying areas.

The trend toward early retirement may stop. "The labor base supporting retirees," writes Joseph Coates of the Office of Technology Assessment in *The Municipal Year Book 1979,* "is declining, and the attractions of full retirement are declining as the average levels of education and material expectation of Americans increase."

There now are 31 retirees for each 100 workers, points out Marjorie Boyd in an article in *Washington Monthly.* This number may increase to as many as 52 per hundred in 2030. What will the figure be in 2000? 40?

The elderly of tomorrow may not resemble those of today. Futurist Herbert Gerjouy points out that those who will be the elderly in 2000 were "at the beginning of the sexual revolution in 1950, may have been involved in the freedom rides of the 1960s, and so on." Thus this group probably will be gainfully employed well beyond age sixty-five, with many living in the equivalent of today's singles apartments.

At a minimum, larger elderly populations are going to strain existing pension and social security systems. They will create high demands for adequate medical care, abundant part-time employment, special recreation facilities, housing programs designed to serve elderly populations, and career retraining facilities. The demands, incidentally, will be economic as well as political; they will affect both private businesses and government.

Those demands made on government, concluded the committee, will be particularly important. Dennis Little of the Congressional Research Service noted that the organized elderly are quickly overtaking local interest groups such as the PTA in exerting effective pressure on local and federal government.

Figure 3 Population Growth: 1790–2040.

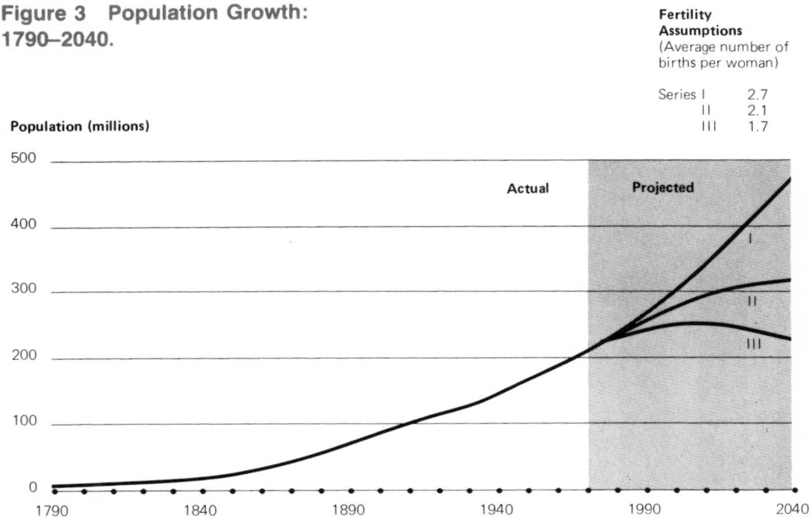

Fertility
Assumptions
(Average number of
births per woman)

Series I	2.7
II	2.1
III	1.7

Population (millions)

Note: Displayed here is the growth of the population of the United States from 1790 (the date of the first official census enumeration) to 1970 (the date of the most recent decennial census), together with three alternative paths of population growth from 1970 to the year 2040, reflecting the implications of three assumptions in regard to the future fertility of American women. Series I assumes the future fertility of women of childbearing age will result in an average of 2.7 children per woman; Series II assumes an average of 2.1 children; and Series III assumes an average of 1.7 children. If current levels of fertility were to continue without substantial change, the future growth of the nation's population would approximate the path shown by Series II.

Baby-boom cohorts

There is much speculation about the ramifications of this aging of the baby-boom cohorts. Speculators have played with several questions: What will happen to these people when they reach the middle of their careers? What will happen by the year 2000?

An alarm has been sounded. The committee saw images of middle management swollen with people who were born after World War II and who have reached their career peaks. It is certain that competition for pay and position will heighten, while advancement will be slower.

"The baby boom cohorts," reports *Business Week*, "are likely to experience continuing difficulties in satisfying career and income aspirations—simply because of the competitive pressures generated by their sheer numbers—just as they had faced heightened unemployment in their teens."

Households

The atomization in American life has equally profound consequences. People are living in smaller and smaller groups, and these groups are breaking up far more frequently than in the past. In addition, the structure of the groups is increasingly nontraditional.

According to *Social Indicators, 1976*, average household size was 3.29 individuals in 1965. By 1975 there were 2.94 individuals per household. Moreover, between 1960 and 1975, the percentage of the population that lived alone, or with people to whom they were not related by blood or marriage, increased significantly; for men eighteen to sixty-four years of age, it increased 35 percent (from 7.9 percent to 10.7 percent of all men in that age group). For women the increase was 13 percent (from 8.3 to 9.4 percent). By 1995, the Bureau of the Census foresees even smaller and more numerous households, with the number increasing between 28 and 41 percent.

Families—people related by blood or marriage—have declined in size as well. The size of families reached its peak in 1965 with an average of 3.7 people. In 1975 the size had declined to 3.4 people. If there is no change in fertility rates, the size will be 3.0 by 1990, according to Bureau of the Census projections.

Powerful social forces lie behind these trends. Divorce is both more common and more acceptable than in the past, the rate having increased nearly 150 percent since 1960. Fertility, as noted already, has been declining. Thus child rearing, a primary reason for family creation, is not as important as it was years ago. Social mores are changing in other ways: unmarried couples live together, homosexuals set up households, and other groups create various living arrangements.

Women

Perhaps the most socially significant factor behind the trend toward atomization has been the growing social, economic, and political independence of women. This independence doubtless is related to the trend toward having few or no children, the increasing acceptability of divorce, and the relaxation of pressures for marriage.

In 1965, 34 percent of the work force was female, compared with 39 percent in 1975. The Bureau of the Census projects that by 1990 the figure will be 42 percent.

Women continue to gain on men in terms of longevity. The gains are so dramatic that by the year 2000, women seventy-five years of age and over will outnumber men in this age group by two to one (8.9 million women to 4.7 million men).

Dramatic increases in the participation of women in the day-to-day economic life of the country are inevitable by 2000. The Conference Board, a prestigious business research group, expects many of the gains by women to be in clerical or service jobs.

China has four times the population of the U.S. within a land area of roughly the same size. With intensive labor, scrupulous conservation of resources and recycling of human and animal wastes, the Chinese are feeding and supporting themselves without outside aid.

Donald MacInnis

Furthermore, writes Karen Keesling for the Congressional Research Service, "women will probably continue to further their education and enter the job market even if they stay home when children are young." She also expects women to work for longer periods of time.

The committee feels that the atomization caused by women's political, social, and economic independence will continue beyond the year 2000, and demographer William Alonso believes these trends toward smaller households and more independent living will go on for three reasons. The first is that "they represent a consistent story that has been evolving for many decades, with only the temporary anomalies of the baby-boom era." Second, these trends are not just an American phenomenon, but are common to all developed countries. Finally, he finds that "these changes are deeply anchored and mutually reinforcing," which is to say that economically independent women tend to want fewer children since fewer children allow women to be more independent.

Race

Another dimension of American demography is race. The Bureau of the Census does not foresee any dramatic change in the overall racial composition of the public. Eleven percent of the population in 1960 was black. In 1970 the figure was still 11 percent, but it is expected to grow to 13 percent by the year 2000.

Figure 4   Average Size of Families, by Age of Members: 1950–1990.

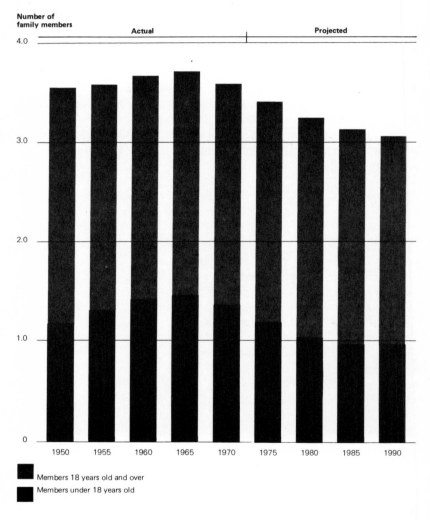

Members 18 years old and over

Members under 18 years old

Note: The average size of American families reached a peak around 1965, largely owing to the "baby boom" of the 1950s. Since 1965 it has diminished steadily and is expected to continue to decline. The bulk of this decline is attributable to the drop in family members under 18 years of age. A return to the higher fertility rates of the 1950s would produce a reversal of this downward trend.

In contrast to the relatively stable black population, the Bureau of the Census and other demographic sources predict major increases in the Hispanic population. Census predictions are that the total minority population in the United States will grow from 13 percent in 1970 to 16 percent in 2000; the largest increase will be in the Hispanic population.

Some demographers predict that by 1985 Hispanics will be the largest single minority in the United States, outnumbering blacks by a considerable margin. The term *Hispanic* encompasses people from Latin American countries: Mexico, Puerto Rico, Cuba, and Central and South America. Some Hispanics, such as young Mexicans, may prefer to be called Chicanos, while others prefer to be called Latinos or Latins. The choice depends to a large degree on their country of origin.

As we know, minorities are not distributed evenly across the United States. Blacks are highly concentrated in the South, as they have been historically—and most researchers agree with Thomas F. Pettigrew, who writes in the *Annals of the American Academy of Political and Social Science* that the South is likely "to remain the dominant regional home of black Americans."

Outside of those living in the South, blacks live in many large northeastern and midwestern cities. Pettigrew notes that in 1970, one out of every three blacks lived in fifteen central cities, a pattern that is likely to be sustained until the year 2000.

Hispanics tend to be clustered in the West and Southwest, although large enclaves can be found from Kansas City, Missouri, to Hartford, Connecticut. One-third of them live in California, mostly in or around Los Angeles, and 20 percent of the population of Texas is Hispanic. This regional distribution, like that of blacks, is likely to continue until 2000.

A demographic map of the United States would place blacks to the east of the Mississippi and Hispanics to the west. In the vast middle of the map would be Native Americans, a small but potentially significant minority.

Thus, the curiosities of today's population become the harbingers of America 2000 and its local citizens:

The over-thirty fashion model, whose mass appeal would have died at age twenty-five ten years ago, is a symbol of youth and beauty to an aging population.

Smaller families signal the growing atomization of the population as we look toward the year 2000.

Women sports writers—who cover everything from the pro football draft to baseball locker rooms—symbolize the extent to which women have become, and will continue to become, independent and undifferentiated economically and socially.

And the high percentage of Hispanic children in the kindergartens of Los Angeles demonstrates the growing importance of this minority in the future of American local governments.

URBAN PATTERNS

The committee believes that the citizens of local governments in the year 2000 will be older, will be living in smaller households, will be influenced economically, politically, and socially by women, and will be more likely to be Hispanic.

Those older people, independent women, households, and minorities will not be distributed randomly across the landscape, of course. There will be distinct patterns, as there are today. The key question is how different those patterns will be in 2000.

The search for a cogent answer is hampered by a number of factors about the patterns of today. First, the image that each individual has of the urban landscape is colored by the person's own experience with that landscape. The best illustration of this systematic bias is a cartoon by Saul Steinberg that appeared on the cover of the *New Yorker*. It is a New Yorker's image of America, illustrating a view from the top of the Manhattan skyline. Once New Yorkers mentally cross the Hudson River, the landscape becomes radically compressed: New Jersey is a thin strip; Chicago is just beyond the hills; Kansas City is a dot on the horizon; and the Pacific Ocean is just beyond.

New Yorkers' visions of urban America are based on their experiences in the New York metropolitan area. People in Los Angeles base their view on that of their metropolitan area. The same is true of Houstonians and of people from Lawton, Oklahoma; Evergreen, Washington; and Cadillac, Michigan. It is difficult to see beyond our environment and our daily experiences. Thus professors of urban politics in Boston create models that fit only Boston, Hartford, and maybe New Haven. No wonder presidents create urban programs that are virtually grab bags for every domestic program except agriculture.

The second factor that makes a cogent description of urban patterns nearly hopeless is the tremendous variety in today's urban landscape. It defies description. Terms such as *urban, suburban,* and *independent* tell us very little about an area. The fact that Norristown, Pennsylvania, is a "suburb" of Philadelphia, and Southfield, Michigan, is a "suburb" of Detroit tells us only that they are adjacent to these central cities. As suburbs, the two places could not be more different. The former is a very dense, old, industrial, and poor community; the latter is a relatively new amalgamation of subdivisions, office buildings, and shopping centers for upper-middle-class residents living in low-density single-family homes. People who know both places intimately will know that even these two descriptions miss a great deal of the complexity and variety of both communities.

The city is not obsolete; it's the center of our civilization.

Edward Logue

There are 38,000 local jurisdictions and 288 Standard Metropolitan Statistical Areas (SMSAs) in the United States, each with a vast variety of human settlements. The differences among them are vast, and any attempt to simplify those differences is destined to do a great deal of injustice to reality. Yet we must try.

Regions

In 2000, the committee believes that the U.S. population will remain concentrated in the Northeast and in sections of the Midwest and Southwest. Also, the shift from the Snowbelt to the Sunbelt will have continued.

A survey of futurists and urbanists by the *Wall Street Journal* recently found that most of those surveyed were convinced that the South and the West will continue to grow for at least another ten years. The growth will be partly at the expense of the older, industrial northeastern and mid-Atlantic regions.

By 1990, Cynthia F. Huston and Dennis L. Little of the Library of Congress Congressional Research Service predict, we can expect a 50 percent population increase in Florida, Arizona, and Nevada; a 37 percent increase in Hawaii; and a 33 percent increase in Alaska. The population in the Plains states, they say, will probably grow the most slowly. "This interregional migration is important, for these migrants tend to have higher family incomes, more job skills, lower age levels, and higher educational attainment than nonmigrants." Moreover, "if population patterns continue in their current pattern and at their current pace, after the next census the southern and western states will hold the majority of seats in the House of Representatives."

Nonmetropolitan areas

The distribution of people between metropolitan and nonmetropolitan areas will change also. There is a consensus among experts for growth in nonmetropolitan areas. Demographer William Alonso has written that 400,000 people were lost to cities and counties outside large metropolitan centers during 1975–76.

The committee, however, is cautious about projecting a change of this magnitude between now and the year 2000. There are missing bits of information, and the phenomenon has only recently been identified. The change may reflect a preference for nonmetropolitan living or a trend of economic activity that is leading workers out of metropolitan centers. It also may be a temporary trend or a definitional anomaly. Suburban sprawl may be reaching into counties faster than SMSAs can be redefined.

In addition, small, independent urban areas have some inherent economic and technical problems that are not easily overcome. A study for the

Figure 5 Projected Demand for New Housing, by Type of Unit: 1975–2020.

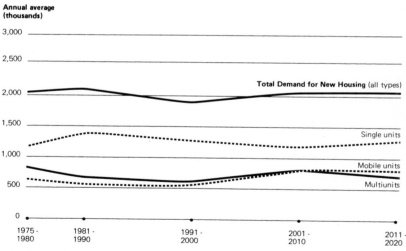

Note: These projections of housing demand, which are based on a computer model of housing demand by type of unit and region of residence using specific assumptions relating to population growth and social and economic change, were prepared in 1972 by Thomas C. Marain of the U.S. Department of Agriculture. They give some insight into the projected demand for units of various types. The Marain projections also recognize the demand for replacement units as well as for new housing units.

U.S. Department of Transportation by the Technology Assessment Group at George Washington University states that "although small towns offer a desirable quality of life, they are vulnerable to the problems caused by high energy costs or shortages. The major transportation problem for small towns is the lack of transportation alternatives for those who do not own automobiles."

Metropolitan areas

Within metropolitan areas, several trends appear to be developing simultaneously. A reordering of populations may be occurring, with the possible result that by the year 2000 these areas will be less dense, with a lower level of suburban growth and new pockets of density. Multinucleated metropolitan areas may be the wave of the future.

The *Wall Street Journal*'s survey of futurists and urbanists found that most believe that the dispersal of the population will continue to the year 2000. New suburbs will continue to spring up, but perhaps not as rapidly as they have in the past. Architect John Kriken feels that the higher costs of traveling from home to work may slow this expansion—yet the suburbs will predominate.

In 1960, the population of the United States was fairly evenly distributed among central cities, suburbs, and rural areas. By 1970, Huston and Little note, "the suburbs had become the most favored locale," with 37 percent of the people living there as compared to 31 percent living in central cities.

"More than half the central cities in the 85 largest metropolitan areas," writes William G. Colman, former executive director of the Advisory Commission on Intergovernmental Relations, "lost population between 1960 and 1973; 39 of the 57 cities having 250,000 or more in 1970 had lost population by 1975."

Overriding the shifts in population has been the emergence of multinucleated metropolitan areas. "Instead of a single nucleus there are now several . . . smaller but often livelier satellite centers along the freeways five to 10 (sometimes 15) miles from the center of the city," writes Gurney Breckenfeld, a veteran writer on urban affairs and an editor of *Fortune* magazine.

Places with a nucleus of high technology and service-related economic activity, plus a wide variety of residential and cultural amenities of high quality, are perfect candidates for such regional centers, writes Gail Garfield Schwartz of the Academy for Contemporary Problems.

When these places are combined with a concentration of transportation facilities and systems such as automobile beltways and mass transit, they are likely to become centers of activity that rival the central cities.

Central cities

After studying trends in urban population movement, the committee recognized that the central city of the future may be just one of several hubs of economic activity, transportation, and residential development.

A likely impossibility is always preferable to an unconvincing possibility.

Aristotle

Does this paint a fairly bleak picture for central cities in the year 2000? It depends to a large extent on people's expectations. It is unlikely that we will experience the kind of revival of older central cities that occurred before World War II, or that our cities will approach the European model of cultural and economic hubs. The much celebrated "gentrification" of older cities such as Washington, D.C., and Boston is hardly a national trend—as demonstrated in research by the U.S. Department of Housing and Urban Development.

Yet elderly persons and those with small households and few children will tend to favor higher-density residential areas, with less emphasis on proximity to quality schools and a premium on low transportation costs. A greater premium on density could foster some movement toward central cities. Joseph Coates points out that "the existing housing stock of such cities is often quite compact and is potentially adaptable to the new equipment [such as retrofitting for solar energy], and is therefore subject to substantial improvement."

Thus central cities may prove to be the modal choice of these segments of the population, but they will be the choice by default of others. For instance, central cities will be the residence of the chronically unemployed who pay little in taxes but use many public services. They also will house a major portion of the minority population. "Even at the accelerated black growth rate in the suburbs during 1970–1974 period," writes Thomas Pettigrew, "it would require roughly 80 years before blacks acquired their true metropolitan proportion in the suburbs." The same is true of the Hispanic minorities and other immigrants into the United States. As Coates writes in

The Municipal Year Book 1979, "Roughly 25% of the absolute increase in population in the United States each year is accounted for by immigration. Immigrants prefer cities; currently some 37% of immigrants have settled in the 15 largest cities. It can be expected that this trend will continue."

It appears that the problems of today's central cities will not vanish in the waves of population redistribution. They may be shared with older suburbs, or with suburban cities and counties, but central cities will have a higher proportion of the poor and of minorities and will have limited tax bases. They also will attract special and growing groups of affluent and mobile or elderly persons.

Nor is there great hope that long-term economic conditions will favor the central city. Even if transportation costs were to go much higher, Gail Garfield Schwartz states that "the costs alone will probably not be sufficient to encourage a return of jobs and people to the city."

Moreover, it is likely that the development of telecommunications technology will produce substitutes for transportation, further devaluing physical proximity to the central city.

So despite the vast variety that characterizes the American urban landscape, and despite the need to oversimplify in order to make generalizations, the committee believes that the urban areas in which local governments are located will experience multiple population shifts between now and 2000:

People will continue to move from the older northeastern and midwestern metropolitan areas toward the South, Southwest, and West.

At the same time, people may be shifting from metropolitan to nonmetropolitan areas.

Within metropolitan areas, sprawl will continue, though at a slower rate. The suburbs will have a plurality of the population, most of it living in multinucleated centers in larger areas.

Central cities will continue to share some activities of the larger areas, but they will be the residences of the unemployed, the poor, minorities, and the elderly; however, they may become increasingly attractive to affluent people with small households and few children.

TECHNOLOGICAL CHANGES
Technology is a three-dimensional trap for futurists. Projections about the future impact of technology tend to underestimate its importance, overestimate its importance, or miss its importance altogether.

Consider these hapless futurists:

"While theoretically and technically television may be feasible, commercially and financially I consider it an impossibility, a development of which we need waste little time dreaming," Lee DeForest, 1926.

"Surface travel will be an oddity [in New York] in twenty years," John B. McDonald, the builder of New York's first subway, 1903.

Consider further these anecdotes offered by Gail Garfield Schwartz of the Academy for Contemporary Problems:

"The historian J. B. Jackson has delighted countless Harvard students with the fact that a grass seed which caused cows to yield more milk completely altered the spatial pattern of New England settlements. The expensive seed encouraged fenced farms and discouraged the grazing 'common.'

"A more universally recognized change in the physical scene was born with the low-pressure tire: by permitting high speeds, the tire not only changed the economics of transport, but also generated the extra-urban commercial strip. . . ."

Consider finally the great emotional response that technology has always generated among people. For some it has been and remains one of the great wonders of life and hopes for the future. For others, beginning with the Luddites of the early nineteenth century and continuing with the advocates of appropriate (small-scale) technology today, it is often an evil and at least a great danger. Technology elicits unbounded optimism, pessimism, or blindness. It also causes great excitement and fear.

Technological forecasts are distorted by all these perceptual and emotional factors. Thus chastened, the committee cautiously reviewed the evidence to find trends that might affect local government in the year 2000.

Seeds of change

Technology promises some important, and yet relatively modest, changes that will affect local government between now and the year 2000. Few experts believe that we are planting the seeds for technological breakthroughs in television or the photocopy machine, but mass transit, cable TV (CATV), solar power, microprocessing chips, and optical fibers may have great impact on cities and counties in 2000.

Mass transit technology is not expected to show any important advances for at least ten years. Henry Nejako of the U.S. Department of

Transportation told the committee that except for further development of small-scale vehicles, today's systems will remain essentially the same over this time period.

Dr. Arthur Goldsmith of DOT emphasized the same point, adding that a great amount of lead time is necessary to design and implement any mass transit system, even one based on the current state of the art. He reminded us of the great cost and political and economic risks involved in such an undertaking. The controversial BART system in San Francisco—planned in 1951 and completed in 1973—was still a subject of debate in 1979.

Cable television is a much different story. Dr. John Richardson of the National Telecommunications and Information Administration, U. S. Department of Commerce, said that we now have the technology for massive introduction of interactive cable television. Forty percent of Canadian households are hooked up to such a system, and at least one major United States experiment in cable TV is taking place. Columbus, Ohio, has a QUBE system that allows viewers to use a console in their homes to communicate instantaneously with people in the QUBE studios.

Solar power also offers important possibilities well before the year 2000, but no technological breakthrough is necessary for its widespread use.

The microprocessing chip is the newest and perhaps the most intriguing technological development for the future. The chip allows incredible miniaturization and economy in the processing of information. In its current form, a single chip, which is much smaller than a postage stamp, is able to do the work that once required a room full of computers. Most of us became personally acquainted with the possibilities of the chip with the introduction of home video games. The microprocessing chip is able to automate a vast number of functions in the home, in the work place, and in the automobile and other machines. A single chip, according to Joseph Coates, can program all functions of the home within a decade.

Optical fibers offer equally dramatic possibilities, although their economic viability is several years away. Essentially the fibers allow a huge array of communication links within a very small space. The fibers look like violin strings and are receptive to beams that can carry simultaneously innumerable communications in either direction.

"What the scientist foresees," writes Erik Barnouw in *Smithsonian* magazine, "is that the virtuosity of the fibers, combined with that of satellites and computers and electronic recorders, will tend to integrate various communication systems and purposes into an extraordinary multichannel, interactive communications world: communication of one to one, one to many, many to one, many to many."

The revolution in our ability to process data automatically will continue through the remainder of this century, says George Lindamood of the National Bureau of Standards. In fact, he told the committee that by the year 2000 we can expect the number of computers to equal the number of people in this country.

This growth in the availability of computers will allow for much greater decentralization of their use, broader applications to social and economic activities, and nearly universal access to them.

In their worship of the machine, many Americans have settled for something less than a full life, something that is hardly even a tenth of life, or a hundredth of a life. They have confused progress with mechanization.

Lewis Mumford

These seeds of technological development, together with current technologies, will be bringing about some important quantitative and qualitative changes—changes that will include the ability to process information, communicate with each other, transport people and goods, and house future generations.

Telecommunications

An increase in communications among individuals also is expected—including a widespread growth in communications among computers and between computers and people.

At least one person expects that, by the year 2000, as many as 100 million households will be connected by cable TV. Joseph P. Martino, writing in *The Futurist* magazine, says that "there will be CATV systems in virtually every town over 2500 population—and in many rural areas as well."

Many of these systems will be interactive, as is QUBE in Columbus, Ohio. More extensive use of optical fibers instead of wires and coaxial cables will allow subscribers and the transmitting station to communicate with each other using fairly complex messages.

Some financial analysts, writes John Wicklein, take very seriously the forecast that movies on CATV will put motion picture theaters out of business as early as 1985.

Another wrinkle in the communications future may be the application of technological developments to computer conferences. Again, Martino is enthusiastic about widespread use of these conferences, which already are being employed selectively.

An important study, *Telecommunications for Metropolitan Areas* by the National Academy of Sciences, raised a number of other possibilities for the future of communications, specifically those between citizens and government. Consoles in the home would provide several levels of communication with the government. Automated information retrieval would allow people to keyboard requests for information about social security, job listings, and other governmental services. Interactive services, such as counseling, also may be available through a combination of computer and CATV capabilities.

THE WORK PLACE   The expected growth in automated data processing and communications promises many changes in the work place. Some of those changes are just now being appreciated.

Coates is confident that word processing already is making the photocopying machine obsolete; and it is limiting the sales potential of typewriters for commercial use. Word processing systems can make it possible for many semiskilled and skilled workers to perform office functions at home. Secretaries may not need to commute to work for a nine-to-five job; they might do their work at home, scheduling their time to meet personal and other needs.

Hollis Vail believes that "the routines of the traditional 9 to 5 office day may disappear completely" with the broad-scale implementation of many of the technological advancements currently used by only a few. Business people on the road today, with a small keyboard and a telephone, can prepare drafts of letters in their hotel rooms, transmit them to their offices, and have them transcribed in final form and mailed at leisure.

Decentralization of work also may be possible, although some, such as Goldsmith, point out that to date experiments with work in the home have not proven successful. Nonetheless, as Vail says, "Computer-conferencing makes it not only possible but *practical* for a hundred or more people located thousands of miles apart to work on the same project and to be in daily contact with each other."

The possibility of a photocopying network was raised with the committee by Stephen Doyle of the congressional Office of Technology Assessment. The network, already in the planning stage, would allow photocopying machines to be interconnected to transmit large quantities of written material instantaneously.

THE PROBLEMS The mass-scale automation of data processing and other forms of communication offers a great many possibilities, but as with most technologies, there are some special problems.

First is the universal problem of controlling the interface between man and machine, as Lindamood told the committee. To a large extent society still has not learned the trick (in the words of Luther Gulick) of *"harnessing technologies to the decision process."* Once we have the data, we do not know how to use it to its fullest advantage. In other words, information is not knowledge, even though it often passes for the same.

A second problem is that of security. Major decisions must be made to limit access to the data stored in our automated processing systems. The privacy of personal information and interpersonal communications remains very problematic.

Anomie is still another problem. The information and communications explosion will probably further reduce contact among people. Increasingly, individuals will interact with machines and inanimate data sources.

The twin problems of privacy and anomie have concerned a great many people, from the authors of *Telecommunications for Metropolitan Areas* to social scientists such as Ithiel de Sola Pool.

In a sense the telecommunications revolution presents yet another problem that may be greater. It is the problem of the unknown.

Let us explain. Insights into social phenomena occasionally come from very odd sources. Some may be slightly undignified, suggesting a lack of serious intent. Some, for instance, may come from novels. Some even may come from novels of detective fiction—for instance, the best-seller by Harry Kemelman, *Thursday the Rabbi Walked Out.*

Speaking of insights leads to a remark made by the leading character in that novel, the rabbi, when confronted with a request to introduce an innovation into the religion. He is reluctant. When challenged, he explains: "Put it down to a natural traditionalism, if you like. If we make so drastic a change, other effects follow, quite unforeseen effects, and some of them undesirable. It's a basic sociological law that you can't change just one thing."

We are not sure who authored that sociological law, but it seemed to fit perfectly with the committee's view of the effects of telecommunications on society.

The fact is that the telecommunications revolution is awaited with great enthusiasm, but it should not be forgotten that when a new gadget, such as a two-way cable TV, is brought into the house, a lot of other unknowns come with it. Thus a great deal of care is necessary to monitor these kinds of technological changes, changes that manipulate the ideas and data being communicated to large numbers of people.

Transportation

In spite of the problems, there is a very real potential for communications to substitute significantly for transportation in the next twenty years. The console may be substituted for the car.

The National Academy of Engineering believes that 85 percent of urban travel is for the purpose of exchanging ideas or information. Such travel might be replaced by some form of telecommunications, but realistic estimates show that about 15 percent are adaptable to a communications process.

Lo! Men have become the tools of their tools.

Henry David Thoreau

The impact that this trade-off might have on energy consumption should be obvious. The effect that it might have on urban configurations is significant. Less obvious perhaps is the importance of such developments on the employability of the handicapped and people who want to share jobs and on the feasibility of dual career families, as Coates suggests.

Transportation will be a slightly less important part of American life in 2000; however, automobiles will still be the major form of urban transportation. At least one study, cited by Robert Maxwell of the Office of Technology Assessment, shows that by the year 2000 we can expect 50 percent more cars, 35 percent more drivers, and 70 percent more miles to be driven annually than today. Many of these cars will be powered by electricity or synthetic fuels, and most will be equipped with antipollution devices.

Mass transit will make a dent in automobile travel, but the decrease probably will not be major without draconian measures to limit automobile use. Mass transit, reports Henry Nejako, will still require public subsidies to remain competitive with alternative means of transportation.

Buildings

A number of technological developments, coupled with economic pressure, will bring about some important innovations in building technology. The net effect will not appreciably diminish the importance of the single-family home or the office building, but it may lead to smaller homes, a greater number of multifamily dwellings, and certainly more energy-efficient structures.

The smart building is coming, say Francis Ventre of the National Bureau of Standards and others. These are buildings whose internal functions would be controlled by microprocessors that allow complex adjustments to changing temperature, sunlight, and wind velocity. They also would perform sensitive security functions such as protecting against fire and burglary in ways much improved over current systems.

Building design also will be affected by the need to reduce energy consumption. Michael deCourcy Hines writes in the *New York Times* about the virtues and potential proliferation of underground houses and other buildings. He points out that underground homes can reduce the costs of heating and cooling dramatically—some say by as much as 50 percent or more. No outside maintenance is required, and underground concrete structures are fireproof and tornado proof and provide good burglary protection. Their density is triple that of houses in the suburbs, yet a great deal of the land could still be used for gardens and recreation.

More mundane changes are expected as well. Coates envisions buildings with fewer and smaller windows. He foresees greater attention to insulation as well. Others see possibilities for buildings and homes to share services. District heating and cooling systems could reduce the need for individual units in each home. This is not a new concept—having existed in Hartford, Connecticut, and Nashville, Tennessee, for decades—but there are signs that people are exploring its adaptation to contemporary needs, according to the *Urban Futures Idea Exchange*.

Outlook

So technology promises some modest, yet significant changes by the end of the century. Computers will continue to proliferate, as will communications, especially through the use of CATV. There will be some tradeoffs between communications and transportation, but the latter still will depend on the automobile in 2000. More automation for buildings can be expected—so, too, can more emphasis on design features that make office buildings, homes, and other structures more energy-efficient.

These changes will intensify old problems and create new ones as well. The most perplexing will be that of "harnessing technologies to the decision process" and to the demands of individual privacy and avoiding the anomie that mechanization and personal isolation can cause.

Yet the committee would be derelict in its duty if it did not end its exploration of future technology by repeating the warning implicit earlier.

Technology is not as easy to project into the future as it might appear. No doubt we have overemphasized some possibilities and underemphasized others. And it is altogether possible that we have left unmentioned other technological factors that will have major impacts on local government in the future.

So as we look ahead, we keep in mind the words of Kenneth Boulding: "I tell my students to be prepared to be surprised, because you almost certainly will be."

POLITICS

Warren I. Cikins sat alone in his cramped Mount Vernon District office at 12:45 a.m., . . . sifting through 600 pages of briefing papers and making notes for his staff on the 14-hour meeting of the Board of Supervisors that had just ended. . . .

Monday's marathon meeting [of the Fairfax County, Virginia, board of supervisors]—a weekly ritual of harangue and bile, of appointments, zonings, sewer discussions, proclamations and corny jokes—was much like every other Monday for Cikins and the eight other members of the board. They call it "tedious," "tiring," "exasperating" and "not fun." . . .

The Monday routine calls for each supervisor to discuss "board matters" first, which means they talk about anything they want. [One supervisor] spoke of a meeting she had attended dealing with bus routes; while she talked, other supervisors ignored her and chatted. "Is anybody listening?" she asked, looking hopefully at the 10 reporters who came to the board meeting in search of stories.

When the nine supervisors finished their board matters . . . [the board chairman took the floor and] said, "When all is said and done, more is said than done."

That statement set the tone for a day in which the supervisors heard about "the criticality of timing" and the "multiplicity of services." They heard angry school teachers, protesting that a proposed 5.15 percent salary increase is insufficient to keep them alive, pounding outside on the windows of the board room. And they heard 23 citizens criticize the proposed 1980 budget. . . .

At 11:07 p.m.—after dealing with the complexities and banalities of county business for 14 hours—the meeting ended.

Cikins drove back to his Mount Vernon district office to pour over his notes "desperately," he said, so as to get home by 1 a.m.

On Tuesday, he went to his full-time job at 8 a.m.

That item by Blaine Harden in the *Washington Post* (April 12, 1979) might have appeared in hundreds of newspapers about hundreds of other city, county, and council of governments boards or councils. The theme would have been the same: "When all is said and done, more is said than done."

What is going on here? Are local elected councils and the appointed officials who serve them unable to conduct their business intelligently, expeditiously, and quietly?

We think not. Councils are as skillful, knowledgeable, and public spirited as they ever have been. More so, in a great many cases. But the job has gotten harder, both for officials at the local level and for elected leaders at the state and federal levels.

The committee observes a pervasive feeling of political impotence among the elected leaders of this country. This feeling is an ominous portent, and, unlike some of the other straws in the wind of change identified by the committee, the trend emanates at least in part from local governments themselves.

The committee asked itself: What are the dimensions of this feeling of impotence—at least to the extent that they are identifiable at the local level? Next it explored the forces that might underlie this feeling of impotence. Finally, it considered the chances that this feeling might continue or even intensify between now and 2000.

Dimensions of powerlessness

Much of what causes elected and appointed government officials to feel powerless can be divined from the story of Fairfax County.

It is hard to forge a consensus among elected officials on the policy issues that confront them. The very length of the meetings testifies to this difficulty. The hearings, speeches, conferences, and testimony on issues are both symptoms and causes of the difficulty nine elected officials have in making a decision. The meeting was fourteen hours long, and from the story we learn that it was typical for this county of over one-half million people. "Is anybody listening?" asked one supervisor.

Officials also feel that even when they make decisions they receive insufficient public support. Who will demonstrate in support of the board's ultimate decision on teachers' salaries? The best the members can hope for is silence.

Elected people feel most issues are no-win propositions. Every issue seems to produce its special interests, pro and con, and much has been written about the rise of special-interest politics. Strong groups are arrayed on both sides of every thorny issue—gun control, abortion, growth—at all levels of government.

At the same time officials at all levels are experiencing citizen efforts to limit taxes and spending, to restrict officials' privacy (through financial disclosure and sunshine laws), or to take decisions out of officials' hands and submit them to the public (through referenda and initiatives).

The result is an increasing disenchantment of elected officials with public service. Cikins, employed by the Brookings Institution in addition to serving on the Fairfax County board, has indicated that he will not seek reelection to office. In 1978 a record number of members of Congress did likewise, citing many of the foregoing factors in their decisions. And one member of this committee, Alan Beals (executive director of the National League of Cities) has expressed concern about increasingly high turnover in local elected officials throughout the country. Most have left office by choice.

All this adds up to a feeling that it is increasingly difficult to get the job done, that decisions are meaningless, that the rewards do not compensate for the punishment.

Dynamics

Many factors underlie this feeling of political impotence, and they cannot all be unraveled here. But the committee identified some major ongoing trends—federalism, judicial intervention, and tax revolt—that may contribute to the feeling. Certainly these are important considerations for local government 2000, independent of their effects on the way political leaders view their jobs.

FEDERALISM   In recent years the federal system of government has undergone some dramatic changes that cannot be ignored by local officials. The changes raise serious doubts about local governments' ability to chart their own courses. The changes are so profound that the committee doubts whether they can be dampened or reversed in twenty years.

The changes in the federal system have come in several waves, starting during the 1930s with the New Deal and the first major series of direct aid programs from the central to the local governments. The late Roscoe C. Martin called the year 1932 a "geologic fault line" in American federalism. Parris Glendening and Mavis Reeves remind us that in the same decade there was "a flood of programs, a number of which circumvented the states and went directly to the cities because of the urgent need to distribute relief funds."

The second wave came with the Great Society. "Between 1964 and 1966," report Glendening and Reeves, "a total of 219 national grants in 39 functional areas were added."

The wave continued unabated throughout the decade. Deil Wright reports that "by 1969 there were an estimated 150 major programs, 400 specific legislative authorizations, and 1,300 different federal assistance activities for which monetary amounts, application deadlines, agency contacts, and use restrictions could be identified."

People count differently—not a surprising fact given the complexity of the system. The authoritative Advisory Commission on Intergovernmental Relations (ACIR) counted 498 grant programs in 1978. And there is not a single example of a program being repealed between 1969 and 1976. (Indeed, the only recent programs to lapse have been the Local Public Works Program and the Countercyclical Aid programs in 1978—and the latter may yet be revived. Both were "temporary" in concept, a rare approach to grant programs.)

Rise above the hope that the federal government will be the source of the energy, the vision, and the resources needed to solve local problems.

George Will

The federal system became more centralized during the 1970s despite much academic, professional, and public discussion about reversing the trend to strengthen both state and local governments. It is an ultimate irony that both general revenue sharing (GRS) and block grants were launched while the federal government in hundreds of ways became more directly and pervasively involved in state and local government decisions. Nobody intended it to be that way, but that is what happened.

The ACIR noted that "decentralization of power from federal to state and local governments was very much in vogue." It was called the New Federalism and brought specific results—GRS and four block grant programs in community development and other areas. These programs were designed to provide maximum discretion for local governments, especially on expenditure decisions, but the evidence indicates that decentralization never caught on. A major reason is that the volume of federal aid, both block and categorical, promoted the centralization of discretionary powers within the federal system. This centralization can be seen from the sheer *fiscal weight* of these programs sitting on top of traditional local programs (police, fire, sanitation, etc.) and traditional local revenue sources (mainly the property tax).

Deil Wright cites data from the U.S. Bureau of the Census that demonstrate the weight. In 1965, cities' budgets were composed mostly of revenue from their own sources—79 percent. Between 1965 and 1975, funds from the federal government grew from nearly 4 percent to nearly 12 percent.

There are other ways to array the data. ACIR figures show that in 1957 the property tax alone accounted for 48 percent of city and county revenue; by 1975 it was estimated to be 33 percent. But federal and state aid combined went from 31 to 43 percent. In other words, close to one-half of local government spending was based on revenue it did not raise locally.

Those data represent aggregates, of course. A closer look reveals why some cities have been dubbed (unfairly, we think) "federal aid junkies." Cities between 300,000 and 500,000 in population in 1975 received an average of nearly 20 percent of their revenue from the central government; some actually received more than 50 percent.

Substantial amounts of this revenue are directly tied to municipal employment. One study by the Brookings Institution found that an average of 12 percent of large city labor forces were supported by the Comprehensive Employment and Training Act (CETA). In some cities the figure was as high as 44 percent, with workers performing critical services: police, fire protection, road maintenance, or administration.

If these billions of dollars could be spent solely at the discretion of county councils, city commissions, and COG boards, it would greatly affect the complexion of local politics. But in no case is the discretion complete. Far from it.

ACIR has demonstrated the great constraints imposed by this national government assistance. Even the most discretionary program—GRS—"is subject to nine specific conditions ranging from filing of planned and annual use reports to using funds within a reasonable period of time." That's not all. Amendments to the program when it was reauthorized in 1976 added stronger civil rights and citizen participation requirements and new auditing provisions. These, concluded ACIR, "potentially constitute a major intrusion into the operations of the 38,000 recipient governments."

The intrusion also is shown in the block grants. Again, notes ACIR: "45 new requirements were added to the *Omnibus Crime Control and Safe Streets Act* in its first eight years."

Categorical grants add an entirely new spectrum of requirements, ranging from union sign-off on transit employees' salaries to the construction of employment exams. Some mandates have been required by Congress; some have come as a consequence of administrative interpretation of laws; and some have been imposed by the courts. At least one study shows that there are over thirty separate classes of national government mandates. And just one class of mandates—for example, the civil rights provisions— might contain dozens of separately mandated activities or policies. Almost weekly in Washington some member of Congress, special-interest group, or administrative agency suggests major new requirements and mandates.

So central government revenue, whether it is 1 percent or 50 percent of local government expenditures, brings with it a plethora of constraints on local officials. In addition, the funds can distort local appropriations to pro- grams and reorient local governments entirely to funded tasks.

Deil Wright offers one example. In the spring of 1976, the director of intergovernmental relations in Syracuse, New York, talked about her job with students of public administration at Syracuse University. During the talk, Wright learned that the director had a staff of eighty persons, which pro- duced $55 million from state and federal sources, or 45 percent of the city's annual budget.

Just one facet of her operation speaks volumes for the potential distor- tion created by federal aid:

[My office] is also responsible for human services planning and program opera- tion. In most communities your human services program operation effort is in a separate department, and that is generally the way it ought to be done. But in Syracuse that's not possible because of the general attitude that local government should be small, invisible, and not involved in extraneous issues. Thus, we operate our human services efforts under the state and federal aid umbrella.

Furthermore, ACIR and others have discovered that elected leaders or general administrators cannot control where national government funds go in city halls or county courthouses: "Categorical grants—particularly project grants—tend to give control to 'specialists' or persons with special area expertise. Elected officials and their top generalist assistants may have little involvement in obtaining, or subsequently, managing a grant." This is true of most block grant programs as well.

Councils of governments also have to be mentioned, for the central government plays an even greater role in the fiscal and policy issues facing the COGs.

Charitably, COGs might be characterized as the linchpins in the inter- governmental system, the key to central, state, and local government interactions. Uncharitably, COGs might be called creatures of the central government.

Deil Wright says that the number of COGs has grown from 91 in 1969 to about 500 in the 1970s. The National Association of Regional Councils counts about 650. Most were fostered by the availability of planning funds from the U.S. Department of Housing and Urban Development under the "701" program and by the requirements of the Office of Management and Budget's Circular A-95 for COG review of all local grant applications.

Many COGs are funded heavily by federal grants. Wright cites as an example one COG in North Carolina: only 10 percent of its budget comes from local governments. A word of caution is in order here. The low local support for COGs is not caused solely by the central government: localities have not put up enough money to allow their COGs to avoid central government fiscal domination.

The money, the mandates, the hegemony of the specialists add up to impotence on the part of elected officials.

Describing a 1973 survey by the National League of Cities, Deil Wright notes: "A more dominant [intergovernmental relations] theme among the mayors (and councilmen) . . . was the shifting of power away from local government." One mayor replied to the survey: "If present trends continue with state and federal bureaucrats making more decisions then local government will become little more than a 'clerical function.' . . ."

David B. Walker, associate director of ACIR, expresses his own views based on directing most ACIR work on the intergovernmental grant system. "In this writer's view these trends and events combine to suggest that the nation has fashioned almost unknowingly a new American federal system with a dramatically changed, . . . complex, and super-charged system of intergovernmental relations which, surprisingly, comes perilously close to unitary rule."

The growth of this unitary system, he adds, has led some concerned observers to believe that it is likely to continue.

Until 2000? It has taken thirty-five years to build, fifteen to mature, and ten to overwhelm. Most of the building took place after 1960. At least twenty years are needed to begin to reverse the trend.

THE COURTS   Another trend parallels officials' feeling of inability to guide the course of local government. But this one may be both a cause and an effect of that feeling.

This trend has been only reluctantly recognized and little explored by urbanists, futurists, and students of public administration generally. One reason may be that it raises thorny questions of philosophy and morality.

Some have called the trend "judicial intervention" or "judicial usurpation" of legislative and administrative functions. Others have called it "legislative cession of power." It occurs when the courts assume functions that traditionally have been the responsibility of Congress, state legislatures, county councils, and city halls, or when legislators give up or fail to assume these functions.

Raoul Berger, constitutional law scholar, is one of the few to have explored the phenomenon in detail, and he views it with considerable alarm. The intervention, undeniably, was initiated by the Supreme Court under Chief Justice Earl Warren. According to Berger and University of Chicago Law Professor Philip Kurland, the Court has used the Fourteenth Amendment to the Constitution as the basis for its authority to intervene. Writes Berger: "It has taken over the policy-making powers of the state legislatures and substituted government-by-judiciary. By resort to the allegedly vague 'equal protection' and 'due process' clauses, it has replaced the choices of the framers by personal predilections of the Justices, which vary with the changing of the judicial guard."

Armed with their interpretation of the Fourteenth Amendment, the Supreme Court—and the lower federal courts and many state courts—have arrived at a string of decisions that may have begun with the powerful *Brown* v. *Board of Education* in 1954 and the one-man, one-vote reapportionment decision of *Baker* v. *Carr* in the early 1960s. Both were decisions of compelling necessity.

The result of these two decisions, now almost universally applauded, has been a gradual, yet pronounced, movement of the courts to deal with issues of similar gravity and national significance.

The problem for legislators is that the issues have become progressively less grave and less nationally significant. The courts not only have mandated scores of legislative and executive actions, but actually have prescribed in considerable detail the process for implementing the decisions. Few if any of the principles can be faulted—certainly not by the committee. Frequently court action has occurred after legislative bodies have let compelling problems fester much too long.

Consider one of the few attempts to catalog this trend:

Courts have taken over the operation of jails in St. Louis, Baltimore, New Orleans, Toledo, New York City, Boston, Jacksonville, Fla.; Knoxville, Tenn., and Lubbock and Harris counties in Texas. They run prisons in Alabama, Mississippi and Arkansas, state hospitals in Alabama, Louisiana and Mississippi, and a school district in Boston.

To operate these facilities, courts have issued orders of great specificity, mandating matters from reductions in institutional populations and increases in staffing to the frequency with which corridors must be mopped.

Similarly, the courts have moved into legislative areas, virtually directing the New Jersey Legislature to enact an income tax, for example.

This catalog, compiled by Martin Tolchin of the *New York Times,* could easily be expanded. The Voting Rights Act, which prohibits discrimination on the basis of race in elections, has resulted in some major judicial intervention in local elections. It has caused the courts to rule that at-large elections are discriminatory and to mandate ward systems in several instances. It prevented Richmond, Virginia, from holding municipal elections for several years. In the case of Mobile, Alabama, a lower court has ruled that the city must abandon the commission form of government for the mayor-council form. In other cases, committee member Norman King writes in *The Municipal Year Book 1979,* the courts have assigned liability judgments against cities for things that once were regarded as acts of God. "Such awards," King points out, "are ... precipitating the overdesign of new public facilities, thereby creating even higher costs for cities."

The committee finds itself looking for the causes of this trend toward judicial intervention. Should it be reversed? Can it?

The search turns up some unpleasant truths for all legislative and administrative officials to ponder. The courts intervene either because judges feel compelled to step in or because they are, in effect, invited.

Let Paul Ylvisaker tell it: "It is no accident that the courts are one of the major instrumentalities which are holding the Nation's feet to the fire. Elected officials rarely can stand the pressures...."

The courts have intervened in school segregation, legislative reapportionment, prison conditions, and countless other issues because judges felt strongly that action was needed—and it was not forthcoming from state and local government.

But in a sense they also have been invited. As Ylvisaker says, "Elected officials rarely can stand the pressures." Increasingly local issues appear to be lose-lose propositions. Feelings on all sides are simply too inflamed. Abortion is one such issue. Others are gun control, capital punishment, school integration, growth versus no-growth, and energy conservation. Even an issue as obviously legislative or at least administrative as whether the Concorde airplane can land at New York's JFK airport became so emotional that legislative bodies shied away from it, leaving final decisions to the courts.

Evidence that the courts are relieving councils, legislatures, and Congress of a great burden is most obvious when the courts decline to intervene. The Supreme Court's ruling in 1977 that Congress and the legislatures must decide whether public money can be spent for abortions is such a case. Virtually no legislator applauded the decision. Most were silent, but the gnashing of teeth was deafening. And as further silent testimony to the anguish, the issue remains essentially unresolved in Congress or in many states.

Looking ahead to the year 2000, the prospects for a reversal of the trend toward judicial intervention are mixed. The Supreme Court under Warren Burger, as evidenced from the 1977 abortion decision and many others, is much less inclined to intrude into legislative activities. But its inclination is ambiguous. Even some very liberal supporters of the former Warren court are beginning to change their views. Some are beginning to feel that intrusion is a two-edged sword. In addition to relieving legislatures of burdens, it cuts in the direction of the ideologies of the judges; and it could begin to have a distinctly conservative turn.

I have never found in a long experience in politics that
criticism is ever inhibited by ignorance.

Harold Macmillan

So a few observers are beginning to question the long-term wisdom of such intrusion. Among them is Raoul Berger, who argues that " 'legislative power' does not become vested in the Court because Congress fails to exercise it."

The prospect for 2000, in the final analysis, probably depends less on the courts than on legislative aggressiveness. If councils, commissions, legislatures, and Congress want the courts stripped of "legislative power," they will have to do it themselves. They will have to act first, decisively, and (unfortunately) with great political courage.

The committee believes that, in spite of the mixed prospects, the role of the courts in local affairs will tend to diminish. The courts will exercise more prudence and legislators more aggressiveness, and some of the most vexing issues of public policy may well be cleared off the legislative agenda.

"TAX REVOLT"   There is another trend that parallels and contributes to the feeling of political powerlessness. In the past it has been given several popular names, among them "Proposition 13," "taxpayers' revolt," and "tax revolt."

The "whipsaw" might be even more appropriate. It does not identify any political movement but describes the effect of a combination of voter attitudes on elected bodies. Councils feel whipped about by seemingly inconsistent yet compelling demands.

The whipsaw or the tax revolt has a variety of manifestations, all very recent in U.S. politics. It began in California in 1978 with passage of Proposition 13, which resulted in some dramatic cutbacks in local government programs and employment. Dozens of similar measures to limit taxes were placed on statewide and local ballots. Some passed; some did not. But few communities escaped the threat of such measures. Meanwhile a movement to require a balanced federal budget took off. As many as twenty-eight states passed measures to require Congress to call a constitutional convention to consider an amendment that would require such a balanced budget.

Responding to the movement, which has a great deal of political support, has been difficult—sometimes impossible. Many of the proposed measures have been so radical that elected officials have perceived possibilities of massive program cutbacks, layoffs, and salary cuts. Each of these possibilities naturally provokes equally strong counterpressures from people served by programs to be cut and from public employees whose jobs are threatened. Likewise, the public provides very little direction regarding the cuts that should be made. Most surveys cite welfare and some social services. But at the local level these often are not significant expenses; and where they are, local officials have found that, in the final analysis, major segments of the public do not want these programs cut. One city manager from California told us: "You know what the hardest programs were to cut in my city? Libraries, closing branch libraries. Some should be closed. But people were rabid when we proposed to close a few. Even my wife bawled me out."

Indeed, it is hard to determine precisely what citizens are saying through this movement. Some have argued that it is simply a movement to reduce taxes. Yet a study by the National Governors Association (NGA) showed no correlation between level of taxation and passage of a tax limit measure in places that attempted it in 1978.

Something more complex is going on. People are clearly frustrated by inflation and its impact on taxes. Inflation is particularly painful in the area of housing, which in some places translates with startling immediacy into higher property taxes. Inflation also strikes through the federal income tax.

As wages go up (irrespective of prices) people are pushed into higher tax brackets and pay a larger percentage of their wages in taxes. (Deil Wright points out that when personal income goes up 1 percent, income tax receipts go up 1.75 percent.) Inflation also produces other frustrations for all citizens. It discourages—in fact penalizes—saving. It produces a false sense of financial gain in wages, but the illusion is quickly discovered.

Citizens also are seriously concerned that the public sector of the economy either is too large or should grow at a slower rate. The concern is more a caution than a demand, expressed in a desire for less government regulation of people and businesses. It is expressed in a reluctance to plunge immediately into another generation of social programs—going from Medicare and Medicaid to national health insurance, or from the current state-run welfare system to a completely national welfare system. Concern for the size of the public sector also is evidenced in expressions of hostility toward current social programs.

Behind the measures to limit taxes, finally, is a wellspring of mistrust, distaste, and hostility that was tapped during Vietnam and Watergate and has been directed toward public officials. Public officials are not alone, however; the same antipathy is focused on corporate officials, doctors, lawyers, and air traffic controllers—to name just a few.

The change in attitudes over the last twenty years was remarked upon by columnist Ellen Goodman in the wake of the nuclear accident at Pennsylvania's Three Mile Island reactor. People seemed to expect corporate and government officials to be lying, she wrote. When officials said things were under control, people did not believe them, perhaps with good reason. In contrast, twenty years ago when President Eisenhower admitted to lying about the U-2 spy plane, everyone was utterly horrified that the president would not tell the absolute truth.

Sadly, we must conclude that behind the tax revolt is a desire to punish public officials, to inflict pain. If decisions are hard, too bad, say the citizens. If it is a no-win situation, good. Do not look to us for help.

We must point out quickly that the feeling is not pervasive. It is largely unarticulated even where we suspect it exists. And it may not be wholly unreasonable: in the last twenty years there have been misdeeds, mistakes, misappropriations, and missed opportunities among officials at all levels. Unfortunately, those officials have provoked hostility that is misapplied to others who had nothing to do with Vietnam, Watergate, or corrupt or deceitful behavior.

Prospects

Public officials are not the only people who feel helpless as a result of the trends discussed here. A large segment of the public seems to feel the same way. In fact, a circular pattern occurs in several phases of American politics today. Central government intervention, judicial intervention, and the tax revolt all pull and tug at each other. The central government stymies local officials; inaction results; courts are invited in; further inaction results; and people decide that in addition to inflation and a lot of useless, expensive programs, they have inept public officials. So they call for central government intervention . . . and so it goes.

The prospect that the resulting feelings of impotence might continue unabated for the next twenty years is sobering indeed. Ten years—five years—would be too long. Yet the prospect is real, precisely because the forces appear to be self-perpetuating.

Yet the circles of reinforcement can be broken, the causes of powerlessness reduced in intensity. A run of improvement—or at least successful adjustment—in the economy would help. We think this is a possibility, as shown earlier. A political cooling-off period, in which all parties stepped back from the fray, would help immensely. It would reduce pressures for judicial intervention.

These changes can be accomplished in many ways. One is for political leaders from the president on down to refrain from overloading the legislative agenda of the country. Another is for experts and activists to reexamine their views for signs of the "Chicken Little" syndrome. Is the sky really falling—or are those just the dark clouds of a passing thunderstorm?

These are neither unreasonable nor unbearable requests for the parties involved. In fact, we see evidence of many people—the president, the courts, Congress, interest groups, the public, state and local governments—calling for similar actions.

So the committee believes that we can reduce the pervasive feeling of powerlessness. But we cannot expect it to disappear between now and the year 2000.

Part 3

Looking
back
to the
eighties:
an interview

Strategies
for the
essential
community

Democratic nations care but little for what has been, but they are haunted by visions of what will be; in this direction their unbounded imagination grows and dilates beyond all measure.

Alexis de Tocqueville

Looking back to the eighties: an interview

Just over twenty years ago—1979 to be exact—a group of urban profes-sionals, experts, and scholars looked at the future of local government. They were the Future Horizons Committee of the International City Management Association.

The committee members tried to forecast changes in cities, counties, and COGs over the next twenty years.

The recommended approach was nurturing the essential community: providing essential services to reinforce the local role in solving national problems, getting by modestly, managing citizen and consumer demand, being skeptical of federalism, and adjusting the scale and mix of services to the urban landscape.

How does this advice stand up today—twenty years later? Your reporter talked to a former member of this ICMA committee recently to explore the history of the last century.

1979 REVISITED

Question. What forces did your committee think would change local government between 1979 and 2000?

Answer. We foresaw vast forces, most of them outside the control of cities, counties, and COGs, but we isolated five that we thought would be most powerful. We called them straws in the wind of change.

Q. Which were?

A. Economic forces (including energy), demographic shifts, urban pat-terns, technological changes, and politics.

Q. Those are powerful forces.

A. Yes, they are. They imposed some major constraints on local governments. We knew even then that some severe economic adjustments lay ahead. Energy would become very expensive. Productivity would lag. So would capital investment. And inflation looked uncontrollable.

Belt-tightening was surely predictable. But there was more. We saw some attempts to limit the growth of the public sector of the economy.

Local government was no longer a growth industry. And we felt it would not become a major growth industry for some time.

Q. But didn't you think technology would come to the rescue? Up to that time it always had.

A. We might have; but those who had studied the issues told us that there would be no quick fixes for our economic, energy, or social problems.

Q. Did you see demography as a constraint on local government?

A. Changes in the number and kinds of people were not necessarily a problem, but we could not predict that the family would suddenly emerge stronger and more dominant. We could not promise that fewer people would be living alone—unmarried or divorced. We felt that the aging of the population would cause demands for new services and reduce demand for existing services.

Q. What about urban patterns?

A. Hopes for rationality here were not very high. Suburbanization would surely continue. The central city would not recover its metropolitan dominance. If anything, it would be successfully rivaled by suburban nuclei.

Q. And regional changes? Did you foresee them?

A. I think so. Older northeastern and midwestern areas—the Snowbelt, we called it—expected to lose population. The so-called Sunbelt would benefit economically. We also saw the possibility of an increase in population for nonmetropolitan areas.

In short, we saw a continuation of the kinds of changes that had occurred for the thirty years after World War II, and we felt that it would be very difficult for local governments to adjust quickly to these changes.

Q. Did you see any other constraints?

A. Yes, political ones. We believed that the central government and the courts would continue to challenge local independence. We recognized that political leaders would be continually whipsawed by demands for lower taxes and more services.

Q. These were serious constraints. Didn't you feel overwhelmed by them?

A. Not at all. We recognized that any look at the future reveals constraints—and at the same time opportunities.

Some of these constraints defined the outer limits of local government. But they gave us plenty of latitude for imagining that local government today would be strong and vital—as in fact it is.

Q. Give us some examples of what you mean by the outer limits of local government.

A. First, we foresaw relatively slow growth for local government. You may recall that the size of city and county work forces and budgets had increased considerably as a proportion of GNP between the mid-1950s and the late 1970s.

We did not believe that rate of growth could continue. The general economic outlook was for relatively modest growth for state and federal as well as local government. People were disenchanted with the track record of government in dealing with problems—and for good reason. Many promises of the 1960s and 1970s had not been kept, especially in the case of urban programs. And local governments shared this failure.

Second, we saw local governments taking on few new functions. Funds would not be available, and people were not enthusiastic about a broader role for local government. But they still were pressing for more attention to the truly essential local services, from police and fire services to sanitation and street maintenance.

Third, we predicted that there would be no technological quick fixes for some of the major problems that beset cities. So we did not hope for miracle solutions to problems of energy, environment, housing, and transportation.

Next, it was clear that the urban landscape would remain as polymorphous as it had in the thirty years since World War II. Metropolitan areas would remain a crazy quilt of people, neighborhoods, jurisdictions, regional centers, and transportation arteries. Rationality would not be imposed before the year 2000.

Finally, we foresaw the continuation of many causes of political powerlessness, a major one being intervention by the central government. We realized that it would be very difficult to keep local government independent, strong, and vital.

OPTIMISM

Q. It must have seemed like an overwhelming set of obstacles.

A. It did . . . at first.

Q. Then what happened?

A. We started to reflect a little on what we knew about the history of local government. We thought about some of the heroes of the first part of the last century and the obstacles they faced.

Q. Who were you thinking about?

A. People like the great reformer Richard Childs. And people like the mayor and city manager who brought Kansas City, Missouri, out of the Pendergast era—Mayor Jack Gage and City Manager L. P. Cookingham. And people like Mayor Richard Lee and development specialist Edward Logue, who led the redevelopment of downtown New Haven, Connecticut. These were just a few examples.

Q. What did you find?

A. We found a surprising thing. They had had it a lot worse than we did—and they succeeded wonderfully.

Q. What do you mean?

A. Well, let me start with one example: Richard Childs. In 1916 the world could not have looked very promising to him—it looked less promising than it did when the committee met. Talk about shifting winds. What about World War I, with Verdun, Ypres, and the fields of Flanders? What about the coming failure of the League of Nations? The *Lusitania*? What about the "shame of our cities"? Tammany Hall?

Yet look what Childs and his colleagues accomplished. The short ballot. The council-manager plan. Reformed local government.

Q. What about Gage and Cookingham of Kansas City?

A. Much the same story. The straws in the wind were much less promising than they were in 1979. Yet these men succeeded in creating out of the Pendergast machine a model of responsive and innovative local government.

Imagine what things must have looked like for both the newly elected mayor and the appointed manager in 1940. Forget the problems caused by the deposed machine for a minute. Think about the Depression; the peak had just passed in 1938. Europe was at war; U.S. participation looked unavoidable. The city itself had festered under a corrupt regime for decades.

Q. And New Haven?

A. Lee had been defeated twice before he became mayor. In 1953 the city was in severe economic decline. The private sector was leaving the downtown. The city's population was increasingly poor, uneducated, and underemployed. The United States was at war in Korea.

Yet Mayor Lee and his deputy Edward Logue achieved wonders in downtown revitalization.

Q. Each success was against overwhelming obstacles?

A. That's right. And frankly they were as bad as, if not worse than, those we faced in the late 1970s.

So we looked squarely into the winds of change and found cause for great optimism. The track record of cities, counties, and the more recently created COGs was very good indeed. Local government had grown enormously since World War II. It had taken on some extremely difficult assignments and had become the focus of a vast number of national issues. Yet we thought it had handled itself admirably.

OPTION: THE COMPLEAT CITY

Q. So the obstacles were there in the late 1970s too. Economic adjustments. Few prospects for local government growth. Few new functions expected. No technological quick fixes. Continuation of the crazy-quilt urban landscape. And the genesis of political powerlessness.

It would seem that you had very few options.

A. We had just three options to recommend to urban leaders. They could seek to become the compleat city—the city-state almost, in the classical Greek tradition. Or they could retreat to the basics of local government. Or they could seek out the best ways of nurturing the essential community.

Q. You chose the last. Why?

A. It was the only strategy that recognized the constraints of the future.

Q. That may have surprised some people. For instance, many had been arguing for comprehensive approaches to urban problems. We all followed Lewis Mumford, who wrote that the city's or county's main function is "the enlargement in human consciousness of the drama of life itself, through whose enactment existence discloses fresh meanings, not given by any momentary analysis or repetitious statistical order."

A. You may recall that Mumford also wrote that "the chief function of the city is to convert power into form, energy into culture, dead matter into the living symbols of art, biological reproduction into social creativity."

The problem is that this image—the compleat city—just was not possible under the forces facing us in the future.

In the compleat city local government deals comprehensively with almost all problems faced by people living in urban areas, perhaps with central government assistance.

The compleat city had been the image shared by many of the people who fashioned national urban policies in the 1960s. In the process, we learned from economist Mark Kasoff that "local government has moved away from its traditional role as a provider of public-merit goods [police and fire protection are two examples] and backed into policies involving questions of equity, distribution and production."

The problem is that the programs to achieve "equity, distribution and production" did not work, and people lost confidence in our ability.

We lost confidence as well when we looked at the forces that might affect American society over the years from 1979 to 2000. I'm talking about economic, social, political, and demographic forces. The problems these forces could cause were too complex, too interdependent, and too universal for local solution.

Q. I'm not sure that's clear. Give me an example.

A. Take housing. The problem of housing was really many problems—most were national, a few local. The overriding problems were inflation, scarcity of well-situated land, an increase in young families buying first homes, the availability of capital, and federal subsidy programs.

Decent housing for all people could not be provided until at least those problems were solved. Local governments, in the meantime, could use their zoning and code enforcement powers to affect the density, mix, and condition of housing stock—but not in the short run. Local governments could administer federal subsidies and loan guarantees—but that was not nearly enough. National government, the private sector, financial institutions, national land developers, state governments, and the schools had to get together on what they wanted.

Other examples that might have been cited were environmental pollution, unemployment, transportation, telecommunications, poverty, and inadequate medical care. In each case cities and counties could help, but they could not solve the problems alone.

In effect, so-called "urban problems" were not principally local government problems. They were domestic and sometimes even international problems that just were most evident in urban areas.

We felt that we had to focus on the essential problems of *local* government—as opposed to national problems that affect local areas.

OPTION: BACK TO BASICS

Q. It sounds as if the committee was advocating a retreat to the early 1900s, when local governments picked up the garbage, put out fires, and patrolled the streets.

A. That was the second option we considered. And rejected.

Q. Why?

A. It too was unrealistic given the shifting winds at the time. The basics do not help in dealing with the overriding domestic problems. Also, many of the functions of local government are more than basics. The *essence* of local government is more than basics.

Q. In what way?

A. Building inspection units that do not understand the need to modernize—to make buildings more energy-efficient and yet not more expensive—contribute to housing problems.

Sanitation departments that cannot efficiently dispose of solid waste in an environmentally sound way contribute to pollution.

Municipal hospitals that create a glut of hospital beds, thus raising the cost of medical services, only hinder efforts to make these services widely available.

Q. Those are some of the basic services. Anything else?

A. Yes. Let's not forget that land use control, zoning, schools, and enforcement of ordinances enhance life style choices and therefore also are essential services for the community.

Q. Community. Don't you mean the population served?

A. Not exactly. Cities and counties serve areas, neighborhoods, blocks, and individuals, helping to maintain or enhance the life style—in fact the diversity—of each. Each is distinct. Each has different needs for land use, zoning, building codes, public behavior, noise levels, permissible air pollution, mix of economic base, transportation, and housing. Areas and neighborhoods range from industrial parks to town house developments; from downtown to older neighborhoods.

All these make up the community served by a local government.

Q. You are saying that the committee felt the basic services were not enough?

A. Right. Governments that supply the basics without regard to greater national problems can contribute to those problems. The basics don't really address the community.

OPTION: NURTURING THE ESSENTIAL COMMUNITY

Q. You eliminated the compleat city. You rejected a move back to basics. What was left, especially considering the constraints on local government?

A. Plenty. Within the constraints, there was plenty of room for nurturing the essential community.

Q. Explain what you mean.

A. Local governments can concentrate on services that help meet both national problems and community needs. That means law enforcement that fully recognizes the sources of crime. Fire protection that emphasizes prevention and reducing loss of life. Sanitation that disposes of pollution, rather than displacing solid waste. Land use controls that preserve neighborhoods, allow for diversity, and provide real choices for citizens. Ordinances that allow neighborhoods to have some choice in the mix of economic base.

Q. Was this possible given the constraints you foresaw?

A. It was indeed. It was the only strategy for local government that allowed it to remain vital, strong, and independent.

Q. Maybe you should explain the components of the strategy.

A. Nurturing the essential community required a number of things. I've already mentioned a few.

Q. There's more?

A. As we saw it, nurturing in the 1980s and 1990s required that local governments learn to get by with much slower economic growth. They had to learn to get by modestly. They had to assist in regulating aggregate demand for services and goods in the community. They also had to be skeptical about support from the central government, even perhaps finding ways of buying back their independence. And they had to learn to adjust the scale and mix of service delivery to constantly changing urban patterns and population. Each facet of this strategy recognized our limitations but enhanced the strength and vitality of local government.

In a period of economic adjustment and slow public-sector growth, concentrating on the essentials in a national context was not only possible—it was absolutely necessary. Citizens wanted and needed the essential services more than ever.

Managing to get by with less—or at least not more—was equally important. Local government had no real practice in cutting back on the vast number of services it performed. It had no practice in being unable to fulfill the expectation that services and government would grow.

Increasing domination of the basic local services by the central government could be forestalled only at a cost. Skeptical local governments could maintain their independence only by buying back what they had lost.

The changing urban landscape permitted—in fact demanded—adjustments in the scale of services.

Q. Could you wrap this up for us?

A. Sure. Nurturing the essential community meant—and means for us in the year 2000—that we work within our economic limits; focus on what we do best; recognize local government's limits; develop services for a much wider range of life styles, communities, and neighborhoods; and adapt to our urban landscape.

Competition of ideas is fundamental to a free society.

William J. Baroody

Strategies for the essential community

How will cities, counties, and COGs go about nurturing the essential community? The general answers were just previewed in a retrospective view of the eighties. But they need clarification. We now must go from generalities to specifics.

The fictitious committee member speaking from the year 2000 said that local governments today, at the outset of the 1980s, and over the next twenty years anticipated the future because "they had to learn to get by modestly. They had to assist in regulating aggregate demand for services and goods in the community. They also had to be skeptical about support from the central government, even perhaps finding ways to buy back their independence. And they had to learn to adjust the scale and mix of service delivery to the constantly changing urban patterns and population."

Get by modestly . . . regulate demand . . . be skeptical of federalism . . . adjust scale and mix to patterns and population. Tall orders.

These are prescriptions for local community actions that seem necessary given the forces of change acting on local governments. They are particularly necessary if we are to maintain a strong, independent, and vital local government.

GETTING BY MODESTLY
Large and obscure words frequently are simply different ways of saying the obvious. Often they are devious ways of obscuring muddled thoughts. But every once in a while comes a word that crystallizes our thinking.

An example is the word *paradigm*. The historian of science Thomas Kuhn used it to mean a world view, but one that is so deeply and commonly held that we hardly know it exists. "Everything is relative, of course," is a common expression—but examined closely it implies a view of reality that is incredibly complex, profound, and pervasive. It implies relativity theory—a world view, a paradigm. Paradigms change. A hundred years ago a statement that everything is relative would have stopped conversation. It did not then reflect the current paradigm of science and life, Newtonian physics. Today Newton has given way to Einstein.

In local government, as in science, there is a paradigm that affects our thinking. It too is complex, profound, and pervasive. It also is largely unexamined and, we believe, is about to change.

Our view of local government assumes future growth. This expectation pervades our thinking about cities, counties, and COGs. The paradigm calls for budgets to grow, federal grants to increase, incrementalism to reign, wealth to rise, roles to expand, and benefits to improve. Nearly every decision made in city halls or county courthouses has been based on the assumption that growth is inevitable.

There's always an easy solution to every human problem — neat, plausible and wrong.

H. L. Mencken

Planners look for new problems to tackle. Firefighters await the next generation of automated equipment. Human services specialists gear up for the next concern, whether it be chronic unemployment, deinstitutionalization of the mentally ill, or lead paint poisoning. Public works departments prepare their budgets in expectation of an incremental increase in expenditures. Police departments prepare for more uniformed officers. Land use plans anticipate growing populations.

As Professor Norman Johnson reminded colleagues on the committee, the paradigm pervades every textbook on government. Every teacher of administrators or public leaders emphasizes strategies for growth.

The paradigm has been relatively valid for the last thirty years or so. Cities and counties have grown steadily and, it seems, inexorably. Local governments were inadequately prepared for a great deal of the growth. Better governments prepare for growth better.

Reality may be outstripping the paradigm, however. Straws in the wind indicate that growth—both economic and demographic—is not inevitable. Holding the line indefinitely may become the order of the decade for public sector organizations. For successful negotiation of the 1980s and 1990s, policy strategies will be based on the assumption that the scope of local government can just as easily contract or remain constant as grow.

Getting by modestly translates into a host of prescriptions for local governments. Some can be identified easily.

Budgets
Getting by modestly will translate into budgeting strategies that are not based on the assumption of incremental growth. These strategies do not yet have names, but they will be in great demand and will be difficult to implement. The difficulty arises because without incrementalism it will be hard, if not impossible, to cover up who wins and who loses—the politics of the shrinking pie. If the pie grows, losses can be masked because everyone's slice increases at least a little even though proportions change. Professor Charles Levine of the University of Maryland is one of the few scholars to appreciate the implications. He calls this the problem of availability of side payments; no growth means it is harder to buy off the losers.

Emerging budgeting strategies must be based on the recognition that it will be much harder to reallocate resources in both the short and the long run. Surprising though it may seem, when inflation is brought under control the problems for municipal budgets will be exacerbated. Inflation at least gives the appearance—a false and pernicious one, admittedly—of growth.

Public/private cooperation
Getting by modestly also will require increased involvement of the private sector in traditionally public sector concerns—meaning greater pressures to transfer services from one sector to the other. Contracting out will be much more popular, but writing these contracts with the good of the public in mind will test local government ingenuity. Private sector support will become much more important in local government decision making. And cities and counties will have an interest in improving the climate for the public sector, especially in the area of unnecessary regulation and red tape.

Science
Modest living requires stronger alliances with the scientific and academic communities. Localities with modest resources need to pay particular attention to advances in scientific knowledge and applied research that promise better services with greater economy. Alliances with scholars and researchers should be in both hard and soft technologies.

Volunteers

The trend toward professionalization of the municipal work force will be halted. Volunteerism will become necessary if not fashionable.

The key to use of volunteers is to distinguish between truly professional and quasi-professional services and between essential and nonessential activities. Volunteers can perform quasi-professional and nonessential services in the interest of getting by with less.

Quasi-professionalism is not the same as unskilled activity. Volunteers can be trained, as thousands of volunteer firefighters can testify. They can perform medical, patrol, maintenance, and other functions on a par with paid employees.

Nonessential activities beg for volunteers—to assist at recreation facilities, libraries, and neighborhood city or county offices and in many human services areas.

Self-help

Another way in which local governments can get by with less is to help people do for themselves what they have come to expect local government to do for them.

This is not volunteerism, where people contribute to the common good, but rather individual self-help, where people take control of their own lives—a control that we project could be even more tenuous in the future. Local government can help people recognize their own skills, resources, and abilities to deal with the problems that beset them.

The problem for citizens is this: They are losing the opportunity to help themselves, to learn about their own capacities to cope and grow. Machines and government have taken over, and we think both will take over more unless checked in the future.

Machines are replacing people in some very personal and sensitive activities. Bank tellers are being replaced by twenty-four-hour banking machines. X-ray machines control access to airport terminals. Vending machines check blood pressure. Disembodied voices tell you when a friend's phone number has been changed or disconnected. Digital radar tells when you are speeding. Police officers on the beat are replaced by elaborate electronic security devices.

Many activities are closely regulated by government. Food, building materials, patent medicines, and clothing are frequently banned because of government findings that they are potentially injurious or carcinogenic. Motorcyclists must wear helmets; cars must have alarms to show that seat belts are not fastened; smoking is banned in many public places. Safety standards, trade and professional licensing requirements, financial disclosure laws, consumer protection bureaus, and firearms registration are among a plethora of well-meant governmental attempts to protect individuals from themselves and each other.

The programs and the machines have laudable objectives and frequently are necessary. But they have contributed to people's loss of control. People remain passive toward the machine, which cannot provide sympathy, cannot be reasoned with, and cannot handle capricious or out-of-the-ordinary activities.

People increasingly assume that their personal problems can, or at least should, be handled by government. But consumer protection is no substitute for caveat emptor. Safety helmets are not tantamount to defensive driving. Safety regulations are not a substitute for prudence.

There is every indication that this sense of powerlessness will increase in the future. The demographic projections for the next twenty years (see Part 2) suggest a real possibility of great atomization—smaller families, fewer marriages, and more divorces. And the growth of telecommunications as a substitute for personal contact (see Part 2 again) will increase the tendency toward anomie among individuals.

At the same time, local governments and the public sector at large will no longer be able to assume a great many social burdens. Surely one solution will be for cities and counties to help citizens themselves shoulder some of the responsibilities for their lives.

Can it work? We think so. The Citizens League of Minneapolis and St. Paul has talked about the need for "supported self-help," the idea that with a little outside encouragement and assistance people can solve many problems for themselves, thus reducing the scales of organizations that would otherwise solve them. With some initial assistance, citizens and commercial establishments can undertake a great many activities for which they may not be willing to pay taxes. They can sweep the streets in front of their homes or buildings, especially if receptacles for the sweepings are readily available. If proper tools are provided, they can trim and spray trees in front of homes or businesses and even maintain neighborhood parks and clean up after their animals. In a few cases local governments have succeeded in changing from back door to curbside refuse pickup, but with considerable protest.

Political and civic leadership is the key to changing the psychology from "this is someone else's responsibility" to "this is my responsibility." And leadership should primarily be by example.

Risk

Getting by modestly also may require coming to grips with what might be called the zero-risk ideal, our tendency to overprotect at the expense of taxpayers. The question to examine is how many public policies and standards for municipal services are based on the belief that the risk of failure or of an undesirable event should be zero. The question is, can the public sector afford to pay for reducing the risk to zero?

This is a tough question—one of the toughest for policymakers. Yet the answers add up to millions, if not billions, of dollars. The reason is that, generally speaking, the cost of going from 5 percent to 1 percent risk is exponentially greater than the cost of going from 10 percent to 6 percent. The closer we approach the ideal, the higher the unit cost of improvement.

Zero-risk policies abound, and many of them are unobjectionable to the vast majority of citizens. Airplane safety standards for commercial traffic aim for zero risk. Redundancy and safety factors proliferate in aircraft design, personnel requirements, and air traffic control. Almost every time a major accident occurs, the ensuing investigation produces changes in the rules—and the cost of the changes is seldom considered. People want no risk, and the huge increases in air passengers (in spite of the substantial cost) show that they are willing to pay the price.

But we must ask tough questions in other areas too. It should not be considered inhumane or embarrassing to ask them, because at the individual level people ask themselves these questions nearly every day. People drive sixty miles an hour habitually, knowing full well that the chance of a fatal accident is higher. Most people do not use automobile seat belts, even though both common sense and research findings indicate that belts sharply reduce the risk of injury or death. People smoke, drink alcoholic beverages to excess, ride bicycles in heavy traffic, go boating without life vests or even the ability to swim, and sky dive in massive numbers, fully aware of the substantial personal risks involved.

Those are personal policy decisions. What about public policy decisions? Can we tolerate a certain acceptable amount of risk in public policies? Does the cost of public safety become too great? Do we make unreasonable sacrifices in the name of risk reduction?

In fire safety, for instance, should we work toward zero risk of property loss? Or is some degree of risk acceptable—provided we continue to reduce loss of life? Is having a community volunteer fire company more important than a certain small loss of property? How much do we pay for a decrease of 1 percent in the risk of property loss? In police protection, how much patrolling would be necessary to reduce the incidence of mugging?

Can we afford the cost? Or is there an acceptable level of risk given the cost?

In each case we need to know the risk involved and the cost of reducing it. We must ask ourselves unpleasant yet important questions: What is the cost of a swing that *no* child could fall off? What is the real cost of making sure *every* public facility is accessible to *every* handicapped person?

The answers to such questions do not preclude a city or county from working toward zero risk. But it may cause them to assess the cost more accurately and appreciate the cost of government generally. It also may make people recognize that they are willing to run certain risks, that such risks are implicit in almost all public policies, and that exposing the public to some risk is not inhumane.

Labor

Getting by modestly involves some important challenges for the public employer and employee. One of the straws in the wind is a reduction of upward mobility generally in the work force. Too many people will be competing for too few jobs at the top.

The new paradigm will require facing up to the fact that within each jurisdiction the possibilities for advancement will decrease. Not every police officer on patrol can realistically hope to become a captain—or even a sergeant. Not every maintenance worker can expect to become a supervisor. Not every administrative assistant can become a city manager.

The problem can be ameliorated only through finding ways to improve working conditions, involve employees in management-level decisions, and encourage interjurisdictional mobility.

Rigid job classifications must be relaxed so that employees can change the nature of the tasks they perform, learn new skills, and have an opportunity for variety if not upward mobility in their work.

Employees who think they eventually will become "management" are more likely to tolerate apparently arbitrary work policies in the belief that they can change such policies when they become managers. With no hope of advancement, frustration over management decisions is much more likely, and efforts to make people feel that they can contribute to these decisions will become critical.

Advancement in the future also will require the ability to move between jurisdictions. Patrol personnel wanting to become sergeants should be able to change jurisdictions to advance when opportunities arise. To permit such mobility, a great many local personnel policies and traditions will have to be changed. Pension requirements will need to be altered. Future entrance and examination requirements should not penalize outside applicants. Department managers will need to appreciate the importance of at least not discouraging mobility among personnel.

All these recommended policies—budget strategies, public/private cooperation, utilization of scientific advances, encouragement of volunteerism, emphasis on self-help, reexamination of the zero-risk ideal, and recognition of the need for alternatives to career advancement—are part of getting by modestly. They are part of the new paradigm. Few of these policies are going to be easy to implement. Yet the lack of growth in the public sector and the economic adjustments and demographic changes in the future make them necessary. They are especially necessary if local governments are to continue to nurture the essential community and thus remain independent, strong, and vital.

Infrastructure

The greatest temptation when trying to get by with less is to defer cost. Some might call this mortgaging the future to pay for the present. It is most tempting when the needs are not visible to most citizens, as in the case of water and sewer lines, underground power lines, and other parts of the urban infrastructure. These are prime candidates for cost deferral. Most citizens are not aware of their existence; yet they require regular maintenance and periodic replacement.

Maintenance and replacement of the infrastructure can be deferred in any given year, seldom with any appreciable effect; but the costs will balloon and become unavoidable. We have learned from work by planners, economists, and others that the infrastructures of older cities and counties are deteriorating at an alarming rate. Huge costs are inevitable soon; yet no annual provision is made to absorb those costs. Each administration, each elected official, each taxpayer is playing Russian roulette. All of them are hoping that the chamber does not fire while they are around.

Newer jurisdictions must recognize this as a problem of the next twenty years, but they need to anticipate it right now. As we know, it can easily take a decade or more to plan and implement any major capital project. Maintenance is an annual process that should not be deferred, even in the face of stern pressures to get by modestly.

REGULATING DEMAND

Some of the same forces—economic and demographic—that will require local governments to get by modestly will also require them to find ways to influence the demand for both public and private goods and services.

"We need to move away from our Western preoccupation with the creation of 'more,' " says futurist Robert Theobald, who spent a day with the committee, "to an understanding of the idea of enough."

We need to understand how the idea of *enough* can be implemented by local governments, how cities and counties can act to reduce both demand for their own services and economic demand generally.

Price

One important and underutilized way to reduce demand for government services is the use of a pricing system. Failure to use prices, writes urbanist Wilbur Thompson, "is at the root of many, if not most, of our urban problems."

A price on a service increases the threshold of use. People learn to think twice about taking advantage of a city or county service if there is a personal, out-of-pocket cost. The cost need not reflect the full cost of the service, but it should be high enough to discourage unnecessary or spurious use. It also causes users to take more personal interest in the delivery of the service.

Prices or fees can be associated with services in numerous ways. Weekly trash pickup may be viewed as a necessity in some communities, twice weekly pickup a useful service, and three times weekly a luxury. It may be possible by imposing fees on a block-by-block basis to allow people to choose the level of service they prefer. Wealthier neighborhoods may want pickups three times a week. Others may be satisfied with a weekly pickup at no charge—the cost being borne by taxes.

The same may apply to police patrol. In Maryland, for instance, the state police literally lease their officers on a county-by-county basis in a "resident trooper program." Some counties are willing to pay for resident troopers; some are not. There is no reason to preclude the same kind of program with municipal or county police on a neighborhood-by-neighborhood basis for patrol purposes.

The price creates a threshold to dampen demand; yet it allows all citizens to receive at least a minimum level of service. Taxes can be minimized and government held to a market-determined size.

Prices also can be used to reduce aggregate demand for consumer and industrial goods and to reduce the side effects of this demand. For example, pricing systems can be built into land subdivision policies to reduce urban sprawl (and the high governmental costs associated with sprawl) and to better control both initial and long-range costs for transportation, water and sewer services, and other services that will be provided in the new area. Much of this pricing is not new; most cities for many years have required land developers to install streets, sewer and water lines, sidewalks, street lights, and other facilities at their own expense for the land within the subdivision boundaries.

A few cities, however, are extending these requirements to come closer to a true pricing system that recovers all costs that otherwise would be passed on to the local government. Examples include: extending outside water and sewer lines to the subdivision boundaries, building fire and police stations, providing school and branch library sites, and paying for off-site improvements such as bridges and connecting roads. A few cities go even further and apply sophisticated cost-benefits analyses to proposed developments to try to measure all direct and indirect costs to the local government. The more precise and complete the analysis, the higher the costs to the developer are likely to be. This may produce intended side effects of directing growth toward the rehabilitation of older neighborhoods where the public facilities already exist.

Pricing also can be used by local governments to reduce waste and pollution, the costs of which are eventually passed on to citizens through the tax system. Instead of building waste treatment plants, local governments could concentrate on placing a price on collection of effluent and solid waste from both residential and commercial establishments, a price large enough to discourage the waste itself. The price could be based on a unit of waste collected.

Two caveats must be offered here.

One is to recognize the complexity of the market system itself, a system in which prices are a prime ingredient. Price levels can affect all facets of the economic system and cause ripples throughout the community. Prices should not be imposed without analysis of the possible consequences far beyond the immediate goods or services involved.

The second caveat relates to equity. Prices can deprive people of services they badly need. Local governments must be careful to use highly targeted subsidies to prevent the very poor from choosing to forgo vital services.

Energy

Energy is the most important area in which demand needs to be reduced throughout society. Local government has a role to play, a role that is part regulation, part pricing, and part leadership.

Building codes need to be updated to reflect community concerns for energy conservation, and they need to be flexible enough to accommodate unanticipated future technological developments. New buildings especially are susceptible to codes that set standards for insulation, site, and types of heating units. Codes can specify that buildings should be capable of being retrofitted for solar energy when it becomes more competitive with oil and electricity. A number of communities, such as Davis, California, have already updated their codes. Others are contemplating such updates.

Codes should emphasize not only energy conservation in terms of heating, but also overall conservation in terms of the amount of energy used in manufacturing the construction materials. This is a new and somewhat controversial approach to energy conservation.

It may be that the process of enforcing energy-related building codes needs to be updated along with the codes themselves. Some communities are using "energy audits," whereby inspectors use visual inspection and/or computers to identify opportunities to save energy costs in heating and cooling. One community in Minnesota uses federally supported employees to help citizens identify ways to make their homes and business establishments more energy-efficient.

Many local governments are directly involved in supplying energy to citizen-customers through their own public utilities. These governments can increase energy efficiency over the next two decades by establishing pricing systems that reduce peak load demand for electricity or penalize users for excessive energy consumption.

A few municipalities have assumed even greater responsibility in delivering energy to consumers. Several places in New England, for example, have greatly expanded their water-generated electric power capacities in recent years.

Many other local governments have taken the view that leadership by the city, county, or COG is an important element in encouraging individual consumption. The new city hall in Vineland, New Jersey, is an example of what has been called a "smart building," with a computer-based system that constantly monitors and adjusts temperatures to conserve energy. Sherman, Texas, has developed a comprehensive plan of energy use designed to help identify short- and long-term conservation opportunities for the city. Springfield, Missouri, has converted a bus into a mobile educational lab, teaching citizens how to conserve energy.

These activities are the wave of the future for local governments as they mobilize to limit demand.

Information

Prices are not the only way to dampen demand for goods and services. Another way is to provide citizens and elected officials better information about the cost of services and clearer choices among alternative service levels funded by taxes. The cost of a zero-risk public policy, mentioned above, is an example. Officials may choose to reduce the risks to zero, but they also may see more clearly the costs of reducing taxes or limiting budget surpluses if they understand the effect of some cost savings on the risks involved. Cutting the budget for building inspectors, for instance, may increase the risk of people living in firetraps or buildings in danger of collapse. Is the increased risk worth the budget cut?

Public education on the costs of services should not be overlooked either. "Don't Litter" signs incorporating some hint of the cost involved might reduce litter and, thus, the demand for street sweeping. The same concept can be applied to all sorts of municipal services.

All these means of regulating demand—pricing, monitoring energy use, and providing better information about the cost of services—will help local governments adapt to an era of getting by modestly.

SKEPTICAL FEDERALISM

Still other strategies for nurturing the essential community should be considered by local citizens, elected officials, and their management staffs.

One is a skeptical federalism, one that contemplates buying back local independence from the national government. It will be no easier than getting by modestly. And it could be very costly.

The committee believes that cities, counties, and COGs run considerable risk of being swallowed up by the central government. They run the risk of losing the ability to determine their own priorities, run their own programs, hire their own personnel, and fashion their communities in the way their citizens desire.

It is conceivable, given the trends described in Part 2, that by the year 2000 most local governments will get substantially more than one-half their revenue from the central and state governments and raise few of their resources locally. Moreover, it is conceivable that if local governments raised no resources independently, the vast majority of their essential activities would be circumscribed by the central government.

Some, such as Professor Richard Stillman II, can imagine local governments that are no more than outposts of the central government, as in some European countries. Their administrators would be employees of the central government. Elected officials would be entirely figureheads for ceremonial purposes. Such local governments would lack independence, strength, and vitality. They would be totally unable to nurture the essential community.

There is only one way to prevent this from happening with any certainty, and that is for local governments to buy back their independence from the central government while they have the resources to do the job.

In simple terms, it is a matter of money. Given the interpretation of the Constitution by the courts, when local governments accept federal money, they are subject to any conditions that might legally be placed on that money. The trend in recent years has been for Congress to impose more and more conditions, and as yet no court has declared a condition unconstitutional. (The most recent Supreme Court case that might appear to be an exception is *National League of Cities* v. *Usery*. The court declared that Congress could not impose minimum wage provisions on local government if no compelling national interest would be served. But the minimum wage was not tied to receipt of federal money; it was a blanket provision. This case probably would not have voided an action that required recipients of general revenue sharing funds to follow the minimum wage, however.)

The more dependent local governments become, the bolder will be the Congress and the president in imposing similar conditions on them.

One image of 2000 holds that Congress will impose regulations on cities and counties regarding zoning, location of adult book stores, textbooks to be used in classes, the caliber of pistols carried by police officers, and the color of fire trucks. The same image has Congress telling local governments what they must do to receive revenue sharing money—when to hold elections, whether councils shall be partisan or not, and what shall be the powers, duties, and compensations for the mayor or chief county elected officials.

This is an extreme image. But it is not beyond the realm of the possible or even the probable for local governments—unless something is done soon to reverse the trends of local fiscal dependency.

A reversal is vastly easier said than done. Short-term political considerations make it extremely difficult to turn down grants from the central government. Yet some way needs to be found at least to make programs, from revenue sharing to historical preservation, less attractive.

Here are a few ideas for consideration by all citizens and local officials.

Taxes

First, locally raised taxes should be made more palatable. The property tax as it is currently structured in most places is a very unpopular tax—and with good reason. The Advisory Commission on Intergovernmental Relations

(ACIR) reported in 1979 that the local property tax and the federal income tax were rated the "least fair" by wide margins over the state income tax and the state sales tax on the basis of a national survey conducted by the Opinion Research Corporation. This dubious distinction has held for both taxes since 1972, and the latest survey (May 1979) showed the federal tax deemed the "least fair" by 37 percent of the respondents with the local property tax following at 27 percent.

It is ironic that a major measure to keep the property tax equitable—annual reassessments of real property—may be the very action that heightens people's perceptions of unfairness. Experience in California and other states shows that annual reassessments force assessed property values to keep in step with market prices and, therefore, with the relentless forces of inflation.

Another frequently cited problem with the property tax is that it measures only the present market value of the property and not the owner's current ability to pay tax on it. Thus, the tax falls most heavily on the poor and those living on fixed incomes, except in places that have some sort of circuit breaker for these groups.

Many people have called for the abolition of the property tax. Yet without it, many local governments would be at a loss to replace that local revenue base and would further lose their independence. And a persuasive argument can be made that land and buildings are an appropriate base for many local taxes and the services these taxes pay for. Many essential local government functions exist for the maintenance and protection of property. Water and sewer services, zoning, and waste collection maintain or enhance the value of property. Police and fire services protect property. Zoning and land use controls and building and occupancy codes regulate the use of property.

The nature, value, and dispersion of property are important determinants of the nature, cost, and intensity of a great many municipal services. A community with all frame homes has different fire suppression and code enforcement problems and services from one in which homes are brick or masonry. Apartments have a police protection problem different from that of single-family dwellings.

So it may not be entirely wise or equitable for local governments to abandon this tax. But changes are needed to make any tax in which property is a factor more equitable and politically palatable.

Cities and counties may want to consider:

A property tax that is scaled to income as determined by a state or federal income tax

A property tax that delays the effects of rapid inflation—and perhaps rapid deflation as well—in land values (income averaging on the federal income tax may be a model for consideration)

A tax that is levied on the sale of property

A tax that distinguishes more between land itself and the improvements on the land.

The fee-for-service concept also needs full exploration by local governments; it uses price to affect demand and is compatible with the notion of public/private cooperation.

A good many services performed by local government are susceptible to a fee structure. The fees need not cover the entire cost of a service, but they should be high enough to generate substantial revenue. The fees do not have to be mandatory, either. Some can be imposed on a residence-by-residence basis, others on a neighborhood basis. The concept is far from new; it is used widely for refuse collection and water and sewer services. But some imagination is required in applying it to other services.

Locally raised taxes can be made only a degree more attractive. But they remain essential to an independent local government. Unless local leaders are willing to take the political risk of levying taxes, they will be levied by others more willing or able to assume the risk. And the price for the risk will be control over how taxes are spent.

Grants

Maintaining a local tax base is only one part of the price of skeptical federalism. The other price is taking a particularly cold look at grants from the central government. Virtually every grant or contract received by a local government needs to be scrutinized. Does it appreciably increase the governing body's ability to serve and nurture the essential community? What are the real costs of the program in terms of the financial management and political direction of its operation? What strings are attached? What forces will be created by the program for local funding once national government support runs out?

The governing body may want to set an annual ceiling on the level of federal and/or state money in the community. And it may want to consider reducing the level of this ceiling annually until it reaches a satisfactory minimum. Every community would have a different ceiling.

Skeptical federalism, in short, means knowing how and when to look a gift horse in the mouth, even when the family thinks the nag is charming—

and then finding the money to get your own mount when the "free" horse looks suspicious.

SCALE AND MIX OF GOVERNMENT

The fourth facet of the strategy for local governments over the next twenty years is finding the proper scale and mix for government services.

Scale

The scale of services has been debated for years. The issue is whether local citizens, elected officials, and professional staff people should work to regionalize and/or decentralize the level at which local government programs and services are delivered.

The answer is that it all depends. The future, we believe, requires both regionalization and decentralization to nurture the essential community. But if there should be a pattern, it will be in the direction of decentralization of local services and programs.

REGIONALISM REEXAMINED   Regionalism is undergoing reexamination. For decades the doctrine among urbanists was that local government should be regionalized. Any step in that direction, it was argued, is a step forward in solving major urban problems.

That consensus has broken down. Now some argue with equal conviction that small is always better, that smaller government is closer to the citizen and can operate municipal services more effectively.

The committee was impressed, but not completely convinced, that small is always better. It did come to realize, however, that many virtues of small-scale policymaking and service delivery have been overlooked. At the same time, however, large metropolitan areas have a compelling need for some regional units and decision-making bodies.

Consider the evidence against regionalism. Academic thought, static for fifty years, is changing, as Irving Kristol points out: "Back in 1952 a committee of the American Political Science Association reported that the merger of cities and suburbs into new political units ('metropolitan governments') was desirable and probably inevitable. Fifteen years later, the newly elected president of the association, in his inaugural address, vigorously challenged the idea that humane and responsible government was possible in a political community of more than 200,000 people."

The whole concept of large-scale urban government is being challenged after a half century of being nearly sacred public administration doctrine. Professor Vincent Ostrom, for one, says, "We have every reason

to believe that where people have access to many different units of government at many different levels of government, they will secure a bundle of
public services that is supplied more efficiently and responsively than if they
were supplied by only one monopoly producer.''

At the same time, we have evidence that the product of regionalism has
failed to sell politically.

Councils of governments have enormous potential for pulling together
into a loose confederation the smaller independent jurisdictions. There are
a great many notable successes. But COGs are relatively new to the game,
still supported substantially by federal money, as Deil Wright has reported
(see Part 2), and still having very mixed success. Or, as Alan K. Campbell
writes, ''Most remain advisory, lack regulatory power, and with a few minor
exceptions, do not deliver services. Their emphasis remains on planning
and the results of their planning efforts can be ignored by the local jurisdictions.''

Large-scale metropolitan reform has been rare in the United States. The
most recent example is in Portland, Oregon, preceded by about a dozen
city-county consolidations and some hybrids such as the Twin Cities Metropolitan Council for Minneapolis and St. Paul.

There is nothing more difficult to take in hand, more perilous
to conduct, or more uncertain in its success, than to take the
lead in the introduction of a new order of things.

Niccolò Machiavelli

The only strong political support has apparently been for the creation
of special district governments. In spite of nearly uniform opposition to such
jurisdictions by organizations such as ACIR and many public administration
scholars, they have proliferated rapidly.

Even when attempts have been made to develop comprehensive approaches to delivering services on a metropolitan basis in the United States,
the urban landscape has changed faster than political opposition can be
defused. Philadelphia and New York City both are products of earlier metropolitan consolidation, consolidation that has been obsolete for decades.

The form of the urban landscape promises to remain too elusive to be
captured by single large jurisdictions in the future as well. Metropolitan
areas of five or more counties are common today; they will be more so in the

future. Most will have several regional centers. Populations will continue to shift outward and back and forth within large metropolitan areas (see the portion of Part 2 on urban patterns).

Finally, many have the strong suspicion that massive, large-scale municipal service delivery organizations promote political powerlessness among both citizens and elected officials. The larger the scale of the jurisdiction providing the services, the more remote it becomes from the individual citizen—psychologically and physically. The larger the bureaucracies and budgets of the organizations, the less they can afford to consider the individual citizen and shape programs for special neighborhood or section interests. The larger the body, the less people can personally identify with the city or county and the elected leaders who make its policies.

The same may be true of elected officials. The larger the jurisdiction, the greater the potential loss of individual efficacy. Competing interests become too large and powerful, better able to stymie controversial actions. The sheer size of the population served makes individual attention to constituencies nearly impossible. (Some councilmanic districts in large cities and counties are larger than some well-known medium-sized cities.)

The result of all this information, speculation, and analysis is that the once unassailable doctrine of regionalism for local services needs reexamination. Regional approaches need to be tempered with decentralization.

LIMITS   The committee foresees limits to regionalism that must be faced. When regionalism takes the form of proposals for comprehensive metropolitan local governments with full service capability, it has at best modest political support, and with good reason. Complexity and grand scale may promote feelings of powerlessness and lack of belonging. There is some evidence that unitary government may not embody the economies of scale once thought possible and may discourage a healthy competition for excellence in service delivery. And where regional approaches have been adopted, they have tended to take the form of special districts that enhance the political problems and introduce some diseconomies of scale.

Yet regionalism, within limits, is necessary. As William Colman, former executive director of ACIR, points out, some way must be found to give citizens more direct control of the special districts to "assure (1) that the public actions of one unit are not permitted to injure the residents of another and (2) that the provision of public services to citizens be financed in a fiscally equitable manner."

As a result, stronger councils of governments are a necessity. Membership must be mandatory, decisions and plans binding, and political leadership support intense. But just as with other activities, local governments will need to recognize over the next twenty years that if they do not take control over these bodies, the control will be imposed from above. Greater central or state government support for regionalism is not the answer. Local support—and this means financial support—is essential. COGs whose budgets come largely from state and national grants and contracts, and whose powers to make political decisions are mandated by state laws or by central government mandates, will be the adversaries of cities and counties.

Local governments will need to budget funds to provide greater support for COGs. The level of support will need to be high enough to dominate COG budgets, and it will need to be relatively consistent over time.

DECENTRALIZATION   The most important trend in terms of the scale of local government services will be in the other direction—decentralization—rather than regionalization.

Colman writes: "Values of citizen accessibility, avoiding the diseconomies of large size, and administration of day-to-day government by small cohesive and informal organizations instead of massive and multi-tiered bureaucracies are hard to argue with. . . . ''

The National Urban Policy Roundtable puts it best: "Some of the deterioration in urban life in America can be traced to our failure to recognize that, for most urban citizens, their neighborhood is the city." The neighborhood, we would argue, is the essential community.

Local governments need to think of the next twenty years in terms of how best to reduce the scale of service delivery organizations. Arthur J. Naparstek, one of the most articulate students of neighborhoods, sees this decentralization taking three forms: administrative decentralization, political decentralization, and citizen organization.

Today a great many cities and counties are experimenting with all three kinds of decentralization. Administratively, the neighborhood "city hall" has been tried in Dayton, Ohio; Boston, Massachusetts; and other cities; the neighborhood planning commission is being tried in Washington, D.C. Politically, some communities are experimenting with having neighborhoods construct their own annual budgets, allocating funds among various services according to their preferences. Citizen groups naturally will focus on the neighborhood, following the decentralization of administrative and political activities.

The objective of decentralization should be to facilitate access of citizens to local government. The scale and methods will vary widely. In a jurisdiction of a million people, access is much more difficult for a centralized government than it would be in one of 25,000. The principles are the same, however. They are to make the government accessible both physically and politically. The specific scale will be different in virtually every city and county. For some the optimum size, as the president of the political scientists argued, may be 200,000. But in a county with 200,000 people, some facets of government may be most accessible and effective at 50,000—or 10,000.

As with regionalism, however, decentralization eventually has limits. Some decisions must be made uniformly for the entire jurisdiction. Major zoning decisions cannot, and should not, be dealt with in isolation; but many variances are only neighborhood matters. The basic requirements for hiring police patrol personnel should be standard; but some neighborhoods may need specialized skills. Solid waste requires centralized collection control, but collection schedules can vary by neighborhood. Overall budget decisions must be made at the city or county council level, but neighborhoods can have many options within the framework of these decisions.

There are, in short, no easy rules. As a general proposition, localities should concentrate on the question of decentralization over the next decade or so. Yet a time will come when they will reach the limits of this important action. At the same time, they cannot ignore the regional picture and the need to strengthen their COGs. But the rules will invariably apply differently in every region and for every jurisdiction within the region.

CITIZEN INVOLVEMENT   One of the important keys to adjusting the scale of government to provide more direct access by citizens is the mechanisms to be used. Traditional methods will still be needed—public hearings, citizen representatives, complaint offices, neighborhood meetings, advisory committees, boards, commissions. But the telecommunications revolution offers added possibilities for reducing both the physical and the psychological distance between citizen and government (see Part 2).

Cable TV is a natural for increasing access. Experiments in Columbus, Ohio, with the QUBE system, which offers two-way communication between subscriber and studio, open entirely new horizons. Cable systems can bring into everyone's home a forum for two-day discussions of vital community issues—zoning, land use, budgets, important ordinances, or whatever.

Cable TV also can allow more direct access by citizens to information from local governments. Video display terminals could be used by citizens in their own homes, or in nearby neighborhood offices, to renew drivers' licenses, check tax records, record complaints, change addresses, request special services, and perhaps even engage in some forms of personal counseling.

There are some obvious, and perhaps unobvious, problems inherent in this adaptation of telecommunications to citizen involvement. Television screens are deemed authoritative by many, as are the numbers that might be used to record reactions of viewers in two-way systems. People have learned to trust television (through Walter Cronkite, for instance) and to take numbers (such as opinion polls) at face value. But there is nothing inherently authoritative about a TV screen. Misinformation can be communicated as easily as correct information. Viewers may or may not be a representative sample—and they may or may not be recording their true reactions. Moreover, there may be a great temptation with these systems to encourage direct as opposed to representative democracy. They could serve to bypass elected officials rather than assist them in reflecting the views of the public.

Another problem is confidentiality. Local governments should be particularly sensitive to this problem because much of the data held locally is of the most personal nature: personal property tax declarations, medical records, and so on.

Mix

Citizen involvement is just one way in which the scale of service delivery should be sorted out over the next ten to twenty years. But the mix as well as the scale of services must be adjusted.

The mix of services provided by cities, counties, and COGs in the next twenty years will be determined in large part by the mix of people they serve. Demography is destiny. As the populations served by local governments change (see Part 2), so, too, will the priorities of the governing bodies.

As we have seen, we expect more people over sixty-five and fewer under twenty years of age. There will be more women, and more of these will be in the labor force. Hispanics will outnumber blacks, who also will increase proportionately, but neither group will be distributed evenly across the population. People will have smaller households and be less likely to be married or to have children.

We only can speculate about the effect these changes might have on local government priorities. But the speculation is important because some of these changes in priorities should be anticipated before they overtake our cities, counties, and COGs.

THE ELDERLY   The specter of "gray power" has been sighted on the horizon as associations of retired people begin to gain local clout. The form such clout will take in the future depends on what makes this population group unique. Will it have a separate and distinct set of needs that local governments can serve? Will it cause distinct problems? Here the committee finds itself of two minds. On one hand, it can identify a number of unique needs of the elderly, needs that will have to be given more attention in the next two decades. On the other hand, it questions whether the definition of "elderly" that we use today will apply in 2000.

Today we think of the elderly as those over sixty-five years of age, because they are very likely to be retired, to live on fixed incomes, to have high mortality rates from disease, and to be approaching the limits of their life expectancy.

It is not at all clear that those over sixty-five in the year 2000 will be so easily categorized. Given the continuing trend toward elimination of mandatory retirement, the fact that life expectancy is probably increasing, and the inability of the working part of the population to pay for early retirement and a sustained income throughout life, it is possible that what we once defined as elderly—sixty-five and older—may no longer fit. It may be seventy and older. Or seventy-five.

If "elderly" is redefined, the population with similar needs will become smaller, perhaps presenting less of a problem than might be imagined today. Nonetheless, local governments will need to begin now anticipating some changes in the mix of services based on the aging of the population.

Transportation is one area of major concern. Greater specialization and flexibility in public transit systems will be a growing need for this segment of the population. The jitney bus, the short-run shopping bus, the subsidized cab may all be in considerable demand. The elderly probably will require this service, because most will be highly mobile, probably gainfully employed part-time, but unable to afford the very expensive automobile fuels of the future.

In housing, there will be an even greater demand for multihousehold dwellings, conveniently located close to shopping and entertainment facilities. The dwellings need not be publicly subsidized, but they will present some challenges, especially in land use planning. It is conceivable that single complexes will be devoted exclusively to the elderly who are dependent on public transportation and who need to be within walking distance of major commercial areas and medical care facilities. This demand may require specialized police patrol and assistance programs and specially equipped fire service personnel.

The elderly, no matter what their age, will have special recreation needs that have been largely overlooked by most local governments. Swings, jogging tracks, and, in some cases, swimming pools may not fill the bill.

Local recreation programs may need to plan for facilities and counseling on more leisurely recreational activities for a much larger population than they do today.

Another problem is clearly pensions. As mentioned earlier, the growth in the percentage of the work force that will be retired in the next twenty years is alarming. Politically and economically it will be very difficult for pension programs to require, as many do today, that current workers pay for the currently retired.

This will hit local governments' own pension programs hard. Those not fully funded now will find it increasingly difficult to shoulder the burden.

The result almost certainly will be that current workers will contribute some more, but retirees will be getting relatively less in the way of retirement benefits. This alone will present local councils with some nasty political decisions. Another result will be that people who once planned to stop working at retirement age will have to return to the work force at least part-time.

Employment opportunities will be one order of the problem, largely for the public sector. But the support services to sustain part-time employment will be a local problem. Transportation has been mentioned. Now we support those who work on a full-time basis by rush-hour bus service and automobile traffic control measures. With more part-time elderly, the non-peak hours of the present will become peak hours in the future. Recreation facilities too may need more flexible hours.

As the elderly increase in number, political influence, and personal freedom, we may see some changes in local politics. Many more of the elderly may be interested in seeking public office, serving on boards and commissions, and presenting their cases to councils. Some observers allege that today's officeholders are younger than they once were. Tomorrow the reverse may be true, thus bringing different orientations, values, expectations, time horizons, and energy to public life.

THE YOUNG We learned that there will be proportionately fewer young people in the year 2000 than today. We can see this happening already, with the closing of schools throughout the country for lack of sufficient enrollment. This was a trend that took most of us by surprise, and we are determined that similar trends should not do so in the future. To that end, the committee urges communities not to dispose of their school buildings and youth recreation centers too quickly. Between 1982 and 1992—depending on what assumptions are made—the Bureau of the Census in *Social Indicators, 1976*, sees an upswing in the number of people under twenty-four years of age. These people will be needing the schools that are being closed today. We strongly urge local governments to consider leasing, rather than selling, surplus space so that it could be converted back to school facilities by 1990.

WOMEN   Women will continue to be a larger proportion of the population than men and to enter the work force in increasing numbers. Their effect on the mix of services provided by local governments will change accordingly.

The day of the woman volunteer subsidizing vital local services is about to end. Local leaders should recognize the growing unpopularity of volunteering among many women, who now are demanding full pay for such activity. This may serve as a counterforce to the desire of local governments to change many services from a professional to a volunteer basis. But as women become more independent and need independent income, they will find volunteering less attractive.

Day care is no passing need. In the future we see day care playing an even greater role in the lives of children than it did in the past. It will extend beyond preschool to school-age children who require care in the early mornings or late afternoons—and to children of mothers who travel on the job or on weekends. Recreational facilities may assume the job of providing day care–type services seven days a week, eight to twelve hours a day, to accommodate the needs of these mothers.

Male underemployment may be another consequence of women's growth spiritually, politically, and economically in society, especially if the economy does not produce sufficient jobs for both sexes. The result, once the considerable problems of personal adjustment are mastered, may be that men will become the volunteers of the future, and campaigns to recruit, train, and deploy volunteers to help the community should begin planning for such an adjustment.

MINORITIES   Over the next twenty years, as today, minorities will be concentrated in certain areas. A great proportion of blacks will be in the Northeast, the Midwest, and the South. Hispanics will be found in large numbers in the Southwest; Native Americans in the Midwest and West.

Affirmative action among all these groups will still be needed, but its implementation in 2000 may be unrecognizable by today's standards. Although we must not slack off our current local governments' commitment to bring minorities into the work force of our cities, counties, and COGs, the new affirmative action will be focused more on preventing slippage and dealing with the problems of people at midcareer, who will then be part of the baby-boom cohort competing for limited jobs.

Beyond affirmative action, local governments will need to be aware of the needs of Hispanics in particular. Language will be the most important problem, as many Hispanics will not speak English adequately to compete in the labor market.

Special efforts will be needed on two fronts. The first will be to make every effort to help Hispanics compensate for language barriers by installing bilingual signs; hiring bilingual local government employees, especially in reception areas; and producing special printed and broadcast material for Hispanic communities. The second should be a strong effort to provide English-language training for nonnative speakers. This will mean incorporating language instruction into adult education and recreation programs and building it into special regular school curricula.

SMALLER HOUSEHOLDS   The declining size of the household will bring about some changes similar to those required for the elderly—the need for multifamily dwellings, for example. Indeed, the change in household size may revamp many of our images of the ideal home setting for a large number of Americans.

We can see the image changing from the half-acre lot with the four-bedroom house and two-car garage in the planned unit development. In its place we can see much smaller homes, many garden apartments, and town houses. We can see people making much more use of recreation and social settings outside the home (since no one will be home in many more cases).

Smaller homes and lots will have several implications for local governments. The number of water and sewer hookups will continue to grow, but the use of these facilities per thousand population may decline. At any given time, fewer homes will be physically occupied by the tenant, making neighborhood security and patrolling by police more important. In some suburbs, with very large houses, there may be more demand to use the houses for "group homes" or even to subdivide them into apartments.

As local governments enter the 1980s and the 1990s, these are just a few of the changes in the mix of services provided, changes brought about by the fluctuating demographics of urban living.

So the mix of local services as well as the scale of their delivery will need adjustment over the next ten to twenty years. This will be another strategy for nurturing the essential community, along with learning how to get by modestly, beginning to regulate demand for services, and buying back independence from the national government.

All this is a very complex, difficult, and challenging agenda for the future horizon of citizens, elected leaders, and their top professional managers.

Part 4

The future of urban management

Management 2000

Reason can dream what dreams cannot reason.

Nicholas Snowden Willey

The future of urban management

While it is difficult to make precise projections, there are some emerging characteristics which may become significant factors for urban governments and institutions in the future.

First, the intense and rapid growth in state and local government over the last 25 years is likely to level off. There are now 12.6 million full- and part-time workers in state and local government. States employ about 28% of this total while school districts employ about 33%; municipalities employ only 20%. (In comparison, the federal civilian labor force has remained largely stable at 2.8 million workers since the mid 1960s.) With the possibility in store of zero growth public budgets, it is likely that the conflict over the distribution of those jobs will increase, with school districts giving up jobs to other public agencies.

Second, it is likely that municipal administration will increasingly require interagency cooperation. Different types of management teams, both formal and informal, will be required.

Along with the above conditions, different budget processes will be developed. There should be a renewed interest in program and performance budgeting. With the new scarcity of resources, demands to monitor the actual work of public employees may increase.

It is also likely that the distinctions between suburb and city will be less sharp. Increasingly, local governments in the context of a megalopolis or a metroplex will find a need for regional problem solving of common problems. The inner suburbs, in particular, will come to share more problems with central cities. Exurban enclaves will be "adopted" by corporate sponsors, who will concentrate specialized industries in massive campus-like complexes away from the congestion and development controls of the older suburban rings.

The political climate will also begin to reflect more substantial inter-generational conflicts. The elderly and retired persons are finding new ways to influence and participate in local government. New problems are emerging among younger teenagers. Adults without children are a larger proportion of the local electorate. Generational differences in life-styles, values, and service requirements will become a more pronounced force in local politics.

Issues of personal conduct are also likely to become topics of local governmental debates. Currently they cover broad areas, ranging from the common use of leisure space and time to new constraints on pet owners in New York City. The designation of nonsmoking areas is another serious issue in some areas. Health and child care are also causing concern. The epidemics of teenage pregnancies and drug and alcohol abuse, for example, are creating many local problems which will become areas of public debate. It is unclear what tensions and solutions may result from these various concerns, but communities may increasingly seek to establish codes of behavior in areas in which there is perceived to be an overriding public interest.

Concern over local election procedures is another growing concern. The interest in postcard and instant registration are examples of current attempts to achieve better participation. In the future, some communities may attempt to adopt mandatory voting such as occurs in several European countries. Other communities may seek to develop a more qualified franchise in which only the "stakeholders" can vote (for example, only parents would be able to vote in school board elections).

Associated with the concerns discussed above, there will be new efforts to manage and affect citizen participation. In the last decade many new approaches to community planning of particular services have been initiated because of federal and state mandates. The total effect of this participation is not clear but, in any case, some participation, especially at the neighborhood and block level, will continue. And as the housing shortage brings more people into large apartment complexes which ring the central city, new forms of middle class organization and participation are likely to emerge.

Women will become much more active and involved in local governance and management. It should be no surprise if by the year 2000 half of the governors and mayors are women. A similar projection could be made for the urban management profession.

Another likely shift in participation can also be identified. This relates to the growing credibility of celebrities and athletes as political candidates. A certain kind of irony exists when public credibility in government is restored when a reassuring figure from the video media is elected to office, endorses a candidate, or promotes an issue.

Finally, it is less clear whether the emerging interest in federal civil service reform and governmental reorganization will have significant impact on the political environment of local governance and management. The need for reform is apparent, and solutions to municipal structures are likely to be attempted—but their success should not be assumed.

THE FUTURE NEEDS OF MUNICIPAL MANAGERS

Given the context of the post-affluent transition and the emerging political turbulence for local governance and management, what are some of the future needs of municipal managers? Several different needs can be projected.

First, there will be a need to master the problems and techniques of intergovernmental finance and budgeting. What has been called "multi-pocket budgeting" is now a complex reality faced by most municipal managers.

The new patterns of intergovernmental assistance will require new approaches to shared accountability. The local program manager may face monitoring requirements from several federal, state, and regional agencies. The "multiple audit" is one manifestation of this system of accountability. In the future there will be a need to shift the emphasis from an enforcement mentality with a concern for minimum compliance to a "coaching" attitude with incentives for maximum performance.

There will also be a need for more effective forms of citizen participation. Oscar Wilde once said that the trouble with socialism is that it takes too many evenings. The trouble with citizen participation is that it may take too many meetings. Managers will need to be able to select time-effective processes of public input if they want high quality and representative participation.

The location, budgeting, and administration of certain government services, particularly social services, are likely to undergo changes. Emerging demands from community-based groups for input into decisions in these areas, and the integration of service provision, will require greater interagency coordination and the removal of federal and state barriers to the commingling of funds.

The rebuilding of staff morale and the development of mutually determined standards of performance will also be required of management at the local level. In the wake of the taxation and spending caps, local government workers will be faced with layoffs, "give-backs," and demands for increased productivity. This will require more constructive approaches to staff development and professional performance.

Another need will be that of orchestrating coalitions among citizens with sharply differing values and life-styles. With some expected decrease in mobility, communities will continue to need to develop a toleration for diversity and social deviation. If there are conflicts, the active involvement of the full community is needed to resolve differences.

The ongoing problems and crises of the post-affluent transition, together with their effects on economic and environmental well-being, will require that public managers have the skills to articulate and interpret the needs of their communities. This will involve the need for new technologies for the delivery of public health and public safety services. Technology assessment and selection skills are likely to become common.

Other needs will be identified as managers address the specific future realities of their communities. Some aspects of the future are likely to be unpleasant. New forms of corruption and new forms of patronage may be forthcoming. New types of community fanaticism may occur. Enclaves of radically eccentric groups may not be unusual in large metropolitan areas.

Every major trend seems to point to a greater degree of municipal governance in the future. There will also be a greater number of sources of input and fewer areas of autonomy in the management of large urban communities. Professional rationality and performance may have to be redefined in order to deal effectively with the new conditions.

Source: Excerpted from Gary Gappert, "The Political Future of the City in the Year 2000," *The Municipal Year Book, 1979* (Washington, D.C.: International City Management Association, 1979), pp. 13–15.

Management 2000

The next twenty years are a time for vision, imagination, and creativity. These decades are no time for illusions about the difficulties inherent in the strategies for nurturing the essential community.

Some will simply ignore the strategies. Inertia will carry many communities far and perilously afield in the future. Some will implement the strategies but find them costly. Some strategies will involve unhappy, albeit necessary, choices. Some people may gain; others may feel they are losing. Gratification will be deferred, perhaps indefinitely.

Implementing any or all of the strategies will require leadership, and the casualty rate among the leaders could be alarmingly high. The rewards for championing these policies are by no means guaranteed to be higher than the risks. Indeed, the career of a leader attempting to achieve the essential community could be, to use the words of Thomas Hobbes, "nasty, brutish, and short."

The leadership of the future will have many dimensions, as it does today, and as it did yesterday. A portion will be political, exercised by elected officials. A portion will be popular, assumed by involved and informed citizens. A portion will be technical, provided by experts in service delivery. And a portion will be managerial, cutting across the political, popular, and technical.

The committee, composed in large part of local government managers and experts in management, found itself focusing on the dimension of leadership it knew best—managerial. In fact, it found the focus irresistible, discovering that a major attraction of gazing into a crystal ball is the chance of seeing your own reflection.

The reflection could prove useful, not only to guide professional managers over the next twenty years, but to help elected leaders and citizens assemble the key strategies for achieving the essential community.

ROLES AND RESPONSIBILITIES

The committee found in its reflection in the crystal ball a number of key features that will characterize the management of cities, counties, and COGs.

One of the most striking features of management in the essential community is that the prime role of the manager will be that of a broker or negotiator—but not a compromiser. The primacy of this role is emerging unambiguously today. Tomorrow it will be mandatory.

There will be many rips in the fabric of local government, created by economic readjustments, population shifts, demographic changes, technological innovations, and political frustrations.

The rips will be aggravated by what was earlier referred to as the whipsaw that threatens many local leaders—the whipsaw of insufficient resources, public apathy, and ignorance cutting in one direction and unrealistic expectations for local government services cutting in the other direction. Citizens are making irreconcilable demands on their local governments—demands, for example, for both lower local taxes and higher levels of service. These demands often are made with a sullen rancor that shows almost no understanding of the dilemmas faced by elected officials in trying to reconcile competing interests. This whipsaw now leads, and will continue to lead, to the potential for profound frustration and finally to an inclination (often acted upon) to walk away from the problem.

Frank Sherwood thinks the whipsaw is an appropriate metaphor applicable to all people in the public service, as he explains in an article in *Public Administration Review*. Public administrators have the responsibility for solving a vast array of problems. That array will grow in the future. But in the final analysis they are not given the authority to carry out the responsibility.

Sherwood writes: "On the one hand, there is the dominant message of responsibility for whatever happens in the domain, enough in itself to generate many guilt feelings. On the other, there is the quixotic assurance that leadership is equivalent to power."

There will be a need for someone to work to mend the fabric in the future. Management may provide that someone. As Richard J. Stillman II has written: "Managers are now and will remain at the delicate fulcrum point where these fierce twin cross-pressures for both narrow expertise and wider citizen representation meet and are balanced." Managers are in a position to stitch up the fabric, binding together the leadership of their communities.

Binding up the rips and taming the whipsaw, however, require some unique skills—skills that traditionally have not been the major focus of local government managers' training. In the past the focus has been on the technology of service delivery, the analytical skills of administration, and the strategies of direction from the top down. In the future, the prime skill of management will be brokering and negotiation.

In a sense the leadership provided by local government management will be paradoxical. It will be the ability to lead by being led, or as Harlan Cleveland has suggested, "to help the followers go where they want to go. . . ."

Management means dealing with incomplete, uncertain information and making the best decision that one can.

Robert Theobald

This paradoxical leadership is far from new or uncommon, as James MacGregor Burns has demonstrated. In the future it will call on the ability to direct an organization or group of people without dominating it. It will call on the ability to help people see their own desires and goals more clearly and (unobtrusively) to help them satisfy those desires and goals. Managerial leadership means quietly instilling in people the belief that they can contend with the future successfully.

In addition to the role of broker, negotiator, and unobtrusive leader, the manager of the essential community will assume a much more important role in the intergovernmental system.

If the strategy of skeptical federalism is adopted in the face of pressures for growing centralization, management will play a central role. The complexity of the intergovernmental arena cannot be mastered by amateurs. Nor can it be mastered in a short period or on a part-time basis. Too many traps, hidden hazards, obscured potential benefits, and money are involved. In relations with the regional, state, or central government, local governments will be relying much more heavily on top professional management for guidance.

Some foresee that this role in the intergovernmental arena may be in danger of going further than this committee believes is healthy. Stillman foresees a day (which managers must be careful to avoid) when the manager is viewed more as a central government employee than a local one because of the extensive interaction with the central government. He sees managers "more as envoys of the Potomac than of Peoria."

Anyone serving as a messenger of bad news is playing a dangerous role. It is one thing for a manager to understand the obligations incurred by acceptance of central government funds; it is quite another for the manager to be perceived as endorsing the obligations or even beginning to identify with them personally.

There is inherent in the position of manager or administrator a good deal of legal authority—appointing key personnel, setting management policies on personnel and procurement, and interpreting the policy directives of the council. There is also the potential for influence through the role of broker and negotiator, and through knowledge about all aspects of local government and the intergovernmental system.

Some might say that such authority and opportunities for influence constitute "power." That may be a useful shorthand description of a highly complex and poorly understood concept, but it should be used cautiously because, as the vast body of serious thought about "power" has shown, the concept is extremely ambiguous and has many dimensions. Furthermore, the "power" to achieve something among people is virtually useless unless the people agree to go along.

The local government of the future will require that management share its legal authority, the influence that comes from the role of broker and negotiator, and the possession of specialized knowledge. Power will be shared.

The distinction between "policy" and "administration" always has been fuzzy. In fact, the very existence of a clear distinction between the two has been the subject of a hot debate among professionals and scholars for years. There is very little consensus about the point where one ends and the other begins.

The distinction will be even fuzzier in the future. Soon, if not already, both elected and administrative officials should concede that they have a shared stake in both policy and administration. Moreover, the demands of organizations in the future will require a sharing of the decision-making responsibility with the top-level management staffs. In both cases, this illustrates what Cleveland wrote about executives of the future, that their leadership task will be "to help the followers go where they want to go...."

A corollary of the sharing of "power" will be the erosion of the firm legal basis for professional management positions, or at least less reliance on that legal basis for the exercise of management authority.

Council-manager government, clearly the best way to provide for professionally administered local governments, has always been defined by its legal basis. ICMA, for instance, recognizes the existence of the council-manager plan in a city or county through analysis of the legal basis for the creation of the position of manager or administrator. If the city or county has a charter or enabling law spelling out the duties and responsibilities of the manager, and if they correspond to the preestablished criteria for council-manager government, the city or county is recognized and listed.

There is no reason why this shorthand form of recognition should not continue. But the committee discovered that for most key decisions, executive actions, and major concerns, the manager of today, and certainly the manager of the future, cannot rely very heavily on the legal basis.

The manager may have the "power" to appoint the police chief, but an appointment without the concurrence of the community and the elected body is potential dynamite. A manager may be the individual who prepares the budget, but to do so without some fairly explicit guidelines from the council and an understanding of the public's sentiments at the time is unwise.

The shift in emphasis has occurred for many reasons. One is that a consensus already exists in many places on the roles of both manager and council, a consensus that supersedes any written documents. Regardless of what the city charter says, some managers involve elected leaders and citizens very actively in the selection of key personnel. In some cases, the politically prudent administrator ends up walking the fine line between recognizing the blurred distinctions between policy and administration on one hand and abdicating a lawful responsibility on the other.

Another reason for relying less on the legal foundation of professional management is that in an era of political frustration elected officials will be much less comfortable delegating authority of any significance. Rather, they will at least tacitly call for someone to broker and negotiate among them for a resolution of either policy or administrative issues.

Lack of job security has traditionally been one of the hallmarks of professional local government management. Professionals in most fields are tenured or virtually so (football and basketball coaches being a notable exception).

The lack of tenure, in theory at least, has been viewed as a necessary counterbalance to the real and perceived "power" of the manager, as well as an assurance of responsiveness to representative democracy.

The committee firmly believes that this calculated insecurity will remain an essential feature of council-manager government in the future. The ability to hire, evaluate, reward, and fire the administrator will be solely at the council's discretion. Fixed-term appointments will not be common; nor will they be considered desirable. Appointments constrained by licensing, certification, or any arbitrary criteria have been used traditionally by many organizations to limit entry and access to a profession or occupation. Managers of tomorrow will continue to resist such impulses, preserving the competitiveness and vitality that are possible only with open entry from a variety of disciplines.

Most managers will continue to feel, along with E. B. White, that "security declines as security machinery expands."

Yet communities should draw a clear distinction between a calculated insecurity and a license for capriciousness. Thoughtless, mean-spirited, precipitous actions can be taken against a chief executive by councils that are completely insensitive to the very real personal, emotional, and financial costs of their actions.

Terminating a manager with no warning or severance pay serves no one's best interests. Failure to live up to oral or written contracts is unconscionable. Publicly airing ill feelings cheapens local government.

Local governments looking well to the future can and will take steps to smooth the difficulties associated with employment of professional managers.

Among these steps will be the nearly universal acceptance of employment agreements between councils and their professional executives. These will not be fixed-term contracts. Rather, like many agreements now, they will specify reasonable periods of severance, encourage attempts to repair divisive misunderstandings, and acknowledge many of the costs inherent in being a mobile professional.

Managers and councils in the future should have access to impartial third parties who will be able to help the council and the manager evaluate each other periodically, make adjustments in their actions, and complement each other where appropriate.

The recruitment process for managers is unacceptably chaotic even after nearly seventy years' experience with council-manager government. It needs to be smoothed out. The smoothness will come through systematic use of outside professional assistance for councils. Such "executive search" can be performed by state municipal leagues and other public organizations, retired managers, and private firms. Even today some such assistance is available.

Councils also need help in establishing workable criteria for recruiting a top professional. They need guidelines for reasonable compensation of a manager, locating the best candidates, weeding out candidates who do not match the criteria, then interviewing the finalists and negotiating an employment agreement with the top candidate.

Too often today, councils perform this function without assistance, even though they have had virtually no previous experience in hiring a manager. Too often this is a prescription for an unhappy and truncated alliance. Faced with the challenges of tomorrow, neither the profession nor the communities it serves can tolerate an amateurish selection process.

The emergence of a new focus for professional management, a focus on brokering and negotiating; on intergovernmental relations; on the interacting roles and responsibilities of the manager, department heads, the council, and the community; and on continued calculated insecurity, will lead to the emergence of a profession *within* the management profession—that of the internal manager.

The committee concluded that the roles outlined above will consume most of the time and energy of top professional managers in the future. Yet there is much more to be done at the figurative "top." In large communities a new group of specialists will emerge to perform what are, in effect, the more traditional roles of management. The scheduling and supervision of multifaceted staff work, from preparation of budgets and financial reports to motivation of key personnel, will fall to the internal manager. The day-to-day supervision of the various departments will fall to the internal manager. Responsibility for understanding the emerging technology of service delivery and appreciating its application to local problems will fall more to the internal manager.

Many communities already have a tradition of a "permanent" assistant city manager, who frequently serves a succession of managers and functions as the internal manager of the city. The city manager in turn works primarily with the council and citizens.

THE QUEST FOR HUMANITY

The Victorian era had its guilty secret. Until a few years ago, local government administration had its own version of the secret. It is no secret now, and with some courage it need not be—it should not be—a secret in the future.

Administrators have feelings, too. They are human; they can be hurt; they feel the stresses of modern life. Managers can feel the same kinds of terrors, inadequacies, uncertainties, and anxieties that beset virtually all people.

That is the guilty secret.

Until a very short time ago, local administrators hid any hint of marital problems and seldom divorced. No one admitted visiting a psychiatrist. Nervous breakdowns were disguised. Boredom, or fear of failure, or frustration was hidden in a cloak of jargon. These very common human failings were concealed from friends, colleagues, and associates. They were hallmarks of a weak professional.

Today this is changing, and every effort should be made to see that the change continues and that localities provide the encouragement for the change.

The promise of the future for any person in a leadership role is a life of increased stress.

Herbert L. Klemme, M.D.

Psychiatrists have become frequent speakers at the ICMA annual conference and at the conferences of countless state managers' groups. In these sessions the profession has begun to explore the secret of its own humanity. Professionals have begun for the first time to face up to the stress that can nearly overwhelm them on their jobs. They have begun to face up to the effects that a highly mobile career can have on spouse and children. They have begun to explore ways in which individuals can come to grips with these problems.

Public Management magazine and annual conference sessions have explored the many facets of the humanity of management. One manager wrote about a nervous breakdown. The wife of another wrote about the stresses families feel when the husband or father is under public attack.

Administrators have begun facing up to this reality. Some have been given support to attend week-long seminars put on by the Menninger Foundation. Others have been able to divorce and remarry (or not remarry, as the case may be) without becoming political embarrassments. Others have treated alcoholism privately and yet with the support of elected officials and associates. A few even have taken extended sabbaticals to recharge their batteries.

These changes, viewed in the light of the history of the profession, are remarkable. They would have been unthinkable a few short years ago. While entire communities were experiencing these changes, they were not thought appropriate for public officials. Now that climate has changed, and the profession is taking advantage of it.

The recognition of managers' humanity should continue. The special kinds of management problems that will arise over the next twenty years require an approach to mental and emotional health that is not beclouded by double standards. It requires an approach that faces up to the fact that administrators, like citizens and elected officials, are human.

THE NEW QUALITIES OF MANAGEMENT

The roles and responsibilities of the professional managers of the essential communities of the future will require some seldom tested skills. Communities should be looking for these skills in the managers of the future.

Negotiating ability

Brokering and negotiating may be the prime talents of the successful manager of tomorrow. Managers will be required to listen carefully, interpret ideas, empathize with many people, and defer personal ego needs. Managers will need great patience and great faith in people's ability to reach agreement and understanding.

In addition, specific techniques, processes, and strategies of bargaining can be taught and acquired. People with this training will begin emerging with greater frequency.

Empathy with elected officials

The future will require managers without a "we/they" attitude toward elected officials. Managers will be required to have great sympathy, understanding, and an intuitive affinity for the needs of elected officials. Managers will have to think like political leaders and be sensitive to their career, personal, ego, and financial needs. To an extent consistent with ethical standards, managers should be able to help elected officials satisfy these needs—in the very same way elected officials should assist managers.

The need for empathy is probably greater today than ever before, and it will be even greater in the future. Elected leaders today are much more likely to follow career paths centered on elective office, much less likely to view themselves as citizen politicians with first allegiance to another calling or profession.

The committee, drawing more on impressions than on hard data, has concluded that people serving on elected bodies focus much of their energy on that body. Many council seats require more time and attention than a person can invest while pursuing another full-time calling. Often the cost of an election campaign eliminates the casual candidate or civic-minded citizen.

For elected people, a council seat is a profession, just as a manager's position is.

Establishing a relationship between a manager and an elected body composed of such political leaders requires great empathy on the part of both the leaders and the administrator. But an administrator may have difficulty understanding and appreciating the values and needs of the elected official. For instance, people attracted to political life are commonly extroverts who enjoy public exposure, while administrators generally prefer to avoid the limelight. Politicians frequently have personal and family ties to a community that go back for generations. Managers generally are strangers the first day on the job, having ties only to their immediate families and having no expectation that their stay in this new community will be permanent.

The management of change is the effort to convert certain possibles into probables, in pursuit of agreed on preferables.

Alvin Toffler

Politicians must learn and understand the mechanics of electoral competition: from precinct organization, through opinion polling and media relations, to familiarity with issues that go beyond the immediate concerns of local government but are politically important, such as abortion or national defense. Most managers must maintain a studied ignorance of elections for ethical and administrative reasons, and their professional concerns seldom extend to such issues as abortion, national defense policy, or methods of fighting inflation.

In a very real sense the elected official and the manager are ships passing in the night, the former off to a higher level of government perhaps, the latter off to another entirely different locale.

As they pass, however, the manager of the future needs to appreciate the special needs of the elected officials and to anticipate similar appreciation in return.

Managerial understanding

The challenges of 2000 will require sophisticated management techniques. These will be the successors to zero-base budgeting, management-by-objectives, and many others of recent vintage. The challenges also will require vast amounts of knowledge—the application of technology to social problems; information and data processing and transmission; and uses of sophisticated behavioral science.

Do not expect the manager of tomorrow to be able to implement these techniques personally, however. Do not expect to find a manager expert in all these areas of science and technology. The knowledge is too great, the skills too diverse, and the time to acquire both too limited to reasonably expect the manager of 2000 to be a Renaissance person.

Look instead for a sophisticated consumer of management analysis and service delivery technology—look for someone who can manage others with the specialized skills.

Awareness of personal needs

Look too for managers able and willing to undertake the quest for humanity. The manager of the future cannot afford to be involved in work to the exclusion of everything else. The manager of the future cannot neglect the familial, spiritual, and physical needs of a complete person.

Look for good conditioning, for managers who know how and when to relax, how to release the frustrations that build up daily, weekly, and monthly, and how to understand and meet the physical demands of the job.

Look for people who know when to call for help. Managers of the future must be unthreatened by counsel and advice, eager to broaden their horizons, willing to take risks, able to laugh off the daily brickbats of public life.

THE CHALLENGE

Truly the next twenty years of local government are no time for illusions. During this time local government leaders, at some cost and risk, must begin to nurture the essential community. Leaders must learn to get by modestly, perhaps without incremental growth in expenditures, but by striving for the following:

More cooperation with the private sector

Stronger alliances with the scientific and academic communities

Greater emphasis on volunteerism

Helping citizens do for themselves what they have come to expect from local governments

Reexamining public policies that implicitly assume a no-risk base

Making local government employment more satisfying

Maintaining the infrastructure

Regulating the demand for government services

Being skeptical about central government support

Reexamining the whole scale of local government

Altering services in anticipation of the demographic shifts over the next twenty years.

Managerial leadership during this period will require the role of broker/negotiator, the ability to lead by being led, a greater presence in intergovernmental matters, a sharing of "power," less reliance on a legal basis, and a career that is no more secure but is less capricious.

But there is one further dimension to the challenge of management in the next twenty years. That is idealism.

The committee was struck by the degree to which the implementation of the strategies for contending with the future requires a profound idealism.

Idealism is no stranger among professional managers. It has been the greatest distinction of this profession, which adopted the earliest code of ethics in the public service and has maintained a record of ethical behavior second to none; but the demands of the future, the potential costs and risks, will not be met without even higher ideals.

The committee views the central ideal as excellence of management. This implies a belief that we can always do better, that we cannot accept mediocrity. It means that we will need to support each other even more than before, that we must look constantly for better ways of solving local problems and be generous in sharing our discoveries. It means that we must all do everything possible to recruit and further the careers of the very best young people ready to enter the profession.

Professional management also must hold high the ideal of representative democracy. In the next twenty years the concept of representative democracy will be seriously challenged. People will lose patience with it during a period of frustration. People will try to tinker with it in the interest of expediency. People will tend to lose confidence in their own ability to participate in democratic decisions.

Yet democracy is the very foundation of professional local government management. Indeed, in many respects the job of the administrator reduced to its basics is to make democracy work.

The concept of equity is also an ideal for the future. The first victim of tight budgets, modest growth, shifting populations, and political frustrations is almost always the concept of equity. Yet it remains an elusive ideal toward which the profession must continually work.

Finally, our commitment to ethical conduct should remain high. Among the proudest achievements of this profession has been its unparalleled record of ethical behavior. By and large, we practice what we preach, and we weed out those who do not. At the same time, we recognize that ethical conduct is not easy or cost-free.

Like Carl Schurz, we find that "ideals are like stars . . . following them you reach your destiny," and for us that destiny is to achieve the essential community of the year 2000.

Appendix A

How the committee worked

The Committee on Future Horizons of the Profession was established in early 1978. Robert A. Kipp, president of the International City Management Association at that time and currently city manager of Kansas City, Missouri, believed that every profession needs to look beyond the immediate present and that it was time for ICMA and the city management profession to take such a look.

A committee of thirty-three members and friends of ICMA was appointed by Kipp. It included managers and assistant managers of cities, counties, and COGs of varying sizes and locations; whites, blacks, men, and women; professors of public administration and policy; national leaders in the field of local government and public administration; and representatives of the private sector.

The ICMA president and executive board instructed us to call on the best minds in the land for counsel and information and to construct the clearest possible picture of the forces and changes that would affect local government over the next twenty years. We sought to learn what choices citizens, elected officials, and their professional management staffs need to make now to ensure effective local government management in the year 2000.

The committee asked the National Academy of Public Administration (NAPA) to convene a group of the foremost public administration professionals in the country to be chaired by Professor York Willbern of Indiana University. We asked Professor Willbern and his group what kinds of questions we should pose, which experts we should consult, and what we might expect from our findings.

The NAPA group met on March 13, 1978, to help establish the framework. This was followed by four meetings of the thirty-three member committee in Kansas City, Missouri: April 4–7, 1978; September 13–16, 1978; January 11–12, 1979; and May 31–June 2, 1979. The Technology 2000 symposium was held in Washington, D.C., on March 6–7, 1979.

Robert Theobald, futurist and social critic; Kenneth E. Boulding, professor at the University of Colorado; Dennis Little, head of futuristic research for the Congressional Research Service; Mark Kasoff, professor at Antioch College; and the late John Osman all spoke to the committee during the meetings in Kansas City.

Each one gave his perspective on the future. Each suggested and worked with us on techniques for moving into the future. There were lively discussions, heated debates, much reading, and scenario building—all dealing with some of the major forces affecting our country and, ultimately, our local governments.

The committee subsequently heard from columnist George F. Will and held a Technology 2000 symposium with experts on the subject from the federal government under the auspices of the President's Office of the Science Advisor.

Elaborate alternative scenarios for local government and this profession in the year 2000 were videotaped to test the reactions of literally thousands of our colleagues and others in the public administration community. The scenarios were used to conceptualize possible futures and to begin to form ideas about how local governments, and ICMA, could contend with these futures.

This report emerged from the process. There naturally is a disclaimer: the report is totally that of this committee; errors, inconsistencies, or false prophecies should not be attributed to the outstanding consultants we employed, nor for that matter to the executive board or any member of ICMA. The report is solely ours.

Appendix B

Five scenarios for the year 2000

The five scenarios set forth on the following pages were used by the ICMA Committee on Future Horizons of the Profession to identify and refine realistic alternatives for local governments in the year 2000, based on five kinds of communities:

Careful Village: A product of a mixture of optimism and pessimism (small, nonmetropolitan area)

Hope County: A product of optimism

Doubt Town: A product of a pessimistic imagination

Delight Community: A product of a very optimistic imagination

Caution City: A product of a mixture of optimism and pessimism (large metropolitan area).

For each of these communities, the committee looked at five broad subjects of concern for local government in the year 2000:

Parameters of urban life: external factors

Government of scale: federalism, regionalism, and other factors of local government structure

Democracy for the twenty-first century: elections, citizen participation, and other political factors

Humanism on a modest budget: education, human services, housing, and other local government services

New reformers: urban executives in the year 2000: political and managerial relations, the profession, and ICMA.

These five subjects make up the framework for the scenarios. Within each subject, the five kinds of communities are shown from left to right so that energy, economy, federalism, citizen participation, and other factors can be compared.

Parameters of urban life

	Careful Village	Hope County	Doubt Town	Delight Community	Caution City
Energy	Plentiful, costly. Regional differences. Alternative sources available.	Sufficient, cheap. Abundant oil.	Scarce, expensive. No alternative sources.	Abundant, cheap oil. New sources available.	Scarce, expensive. Some alternative sources available.
Economy	Decline in living standard. Frugality. Lower productivity. Smaller public sector. Dollar further devalued. High unemployment.	Relative prosperity. Low unemployment. Less poverty.	Bleak. No real growth. High inflation. Shortages of key goods. Major corporations dominate.	Higher living standard. Stability. Little poverty.	Relative prosperity after some decline. Major corporations dominate.
Society	Family intact. No major changes. Organized religion unchanged. Sexual mores stress more freedom.	Society more complex, more spiritual. New life style: conservation.	Families stronger, many extended. Escapism. Drugs and alcohol. Social disruptions.	Family significant. More single people. Organized religion flourishes. Sexual mores conservative.	Family intact. No major changes. Organized religion unchanged. Sexual mores stress more freedom.

Demographics

Population older. Minorities increased.	More older, single people. Smaller families.	Increase in people 55 and older. Women outnumber men 3 to 2. Single people increase. Sunbelt move continues.	Hispanics increased. Blacks constant. Older population, but concept of "age" changes. Retirement at 70.	Shift to Sunbelt. Population in small, freestanding cities.

Values

Less consumerism; nonmaterial values. More religious. High tolerance, more life styles. Less work ethic.	Qualitative, rather than quantitative. Management. Simpler life style. Tolerance of diversity.	Frugality. Less hope. Independence. Self-centered. Loss of faith in science and technology.	Racial equality. Spiritual values.	Conservation ethic. Disenchantment with government and large institutions, but attitudes improving. More individual freedom. More diversity. More egalitarianism.

Communications and transportation

More mass transit, small cars. Air travel cheap. Cable TV, major two-way devices. Mass access to computers.	More expensive. Communications displacing transportation. Threat of mass control.	No major innovations. Communications do not replace transportation. Less demand for mass transit. No increase in air travel. Major emphasis: repair highways.	Mass transit less expensive; cars more so. Communications cheap, thus displacing transit. Home computers, two-way cable TV.	Greater emphasis on mass transit; little on cars and trucks.

Government of scale

	Careful Village	Hope County	Doubt Town	Delight Community	Caution City
Federalism	Authority shifts to regions, states, and feds. All human services to feds. Regional government bodies mandatory.	Balance. Functions sorted out. No increase in government spending. Less reliance on sweeping programs. Government does less but better. Increase in economic regulation.	Strong centralization. Local government a federal outpost. Autocratic politics. Uniformity.	Public sector grows. Increase in quasi-public sector. Grants-in-aid less, but general revenue sharing much higher. States major actors in helping localities. Feds take hands off with localities. Education, health, welfare all federal.	Local power erodes. Local government delivery agent for federal human services.
Regionalism	Regional government displaces local government. Regional arrangements mandated by states and feds.	Stronger regional bodies. Directly elected boards. Limited kinds of issues, but more authority to resolve these issues.	Less important. Much intrametropolitan conflict.	Regional bodies replace COGs; mandatory membership, service delivery, regulatory authority. Traditional services remain with localities.	Regional governments increase.

Size and role of local government

Cities/counties lose much autonomy to regions. Locals regulate values and life styles.	Smaller in population. Some consolidation. Services are more targeted. Less hardware; more human services. Emphasis on referral rather than service delivery.	Poorly equipped; fewer resources. No major reforms in form or scope. Large cities deteriorate. Most cities have infrastructure problems. No leisure services, branch libraries. Social services reduced.	Geographic scale unchanged. A few metropolitan government experiments; two-tiered model most popular. Array of local services same; focus on enforcement of community values. Maintaining local infrastructure is major concern.	No major changes from 1970s. More housing and older adults programs.

Neighborhood

Structure primitive; focus most on citizen interest.	Stronger organizations, some even subgovernments. New decision tools.	Not important in local politics.	Not any more important politically than in 1970s.	More organized and politically sophisticated. Quasi-official bodies.

Public/private cooperation

No increase.	Expanded linkages.	Modest amount of private capital available. Only source of discretionary resources for local governments.	Growth in quasi-public sector. Little growth of private investment in public projects.	Distrust of private sector. More regulation. Little private capital for public purposes.

Democracy for the twenty-first century

	Careful Village	Hope County	Doubt Town	Delight Community	Caution City
Elected officials	Councils elected by wards. No consensus politics. Apathy widespread. Special interests dominate. High turnover for elected officials.	More full-time by wards. Emphasis on capacity building. Thus: more knowledgeable, able, professional. Loss of privacy.	Leadership void. Narrow focus; ward elections. Competition for resources; no willingness to accommodate. Tenure shorter.	Rise of the "citizen" politician. Less election by wards. Greater public confidence. Less use of referenda and initiatives. Political parties play small role.	Decline in quality. More single-issue candidates. Few decisions made by councils. Most by direct popular vote. Greater personal staff.
Citizen participation	Disillusionment with "citizen participation." Few innovations survive. Alarm at power of special interests.	More opportunities due to better communications devices.	Little desire for rational participation, by either citizens or elected officials. Traditional participation devices seen as sham.	Demands for direct participation less. Voter turnout for elections higher. Great use of two-way cable TV for local politics.	Increased. Few decisions without public vote.
Public employees	Largely unionized and militant. Few national unions. Bargaining on management issues. "True merit" concept. Increased mechanization of clerical and other functions.	More resources for public employees: midcareer development, skills development, job upgrading.	No increase in unions, but rise in militancy. Badly underpaid. Unacceptable level of strikes, walkouts, absenteeism, etc.	Elite of local labor market. Higher pay and benefits. National unions have not increased, but statewide unions important. Prevented from engaging in local politics.	All unionized. Strong national unions. Bargaining directly between nationals and reps of local government. No increase in strikes.

Taxation and finance Lower public expenditures. Local governments raise little revenue directly.	Property tax main source of revenue, but many reforms. Sales and wage taxes up; no increase in service charges.	Most local revenue from property or sales taxes, but federal money equals 150% of local with many strings attached.	Heavier reliance on service charges, but not abolition of property tax, just reform. Less reliance on single sources of funding. Less need for direct federal support.	Local government no longer major tax collector. Mostly federal and state taxes and revenues.
Minorities Affirmative action routine. Major issues are between social classes.	Major concern for local governments. Affirmative action still needed. Concern also for women, homosexuals, handicapped, elderly, educationally disadvantaged, and under-skilled.	Now "two nations." Majority rule replaces affirmative action.	Affirmative action unnecessary. Great economic and social progress for minorities.	Affirmative action still necessary. No progress in extending protection beyond racial minorities and women to the aged, handicapped, and other groups.
Elderly Major political force. Major program area.	People work longer. Less pension pressure. Fewer programs targeted for elderly, but existing ones more sensitive.	Major political problem, few solutions. Militant, but dependent.	Redefinition of "elderly" has diminished emphasis on gray power. Elderly in job market longer. Greater need for job retraining.	Dominant political and social group. Many special government programs established.

Humanism on a modest budget

	Careful Village	Hope County	Doubt Town	Delight Community	Caution City
Education	Reduced funding. Innovation in funding: public school "tuition." Concern of regional bodies.	Less subsidization. Use of vouchers.	Less support for education. Public schools: "education of last resort."	Fewer students in public schools. Federal support for private schools. Curriculum specialization. Regional school bodies control.	State and federal funds. Direct local government control.
Pensions		Reduced benefits and liabilities due to rise in retirement age.	Enormous financial burden for all levels of government. Pension plans "own" some localities.	Less pressure on pensions due to longer stay in work force. Stronger social security.	
Environmental protection	Progress made, but much to be done. Energy efficiency in construction. Waste water problems abated. Solid waste on regional basis. Open space hot issue.	Still concerned, but expense of protection down. Selective deterioration.	No longer major concern. People feel they cannot afford the cost.	Permanent and dominant role for government. People willing to pay the cost. Recycling major disposal method. Land use controlled on regional basis.	Less public concern.

Public safety Violent crime down; political crime up. Emphasis on crime prevention and corrections.	Increase in violent crime. No move to decriminalize "victimless" crimes. More money to courts and corrections.	No longer major concern. People cannot afford the cost.	Shift from traditional concerns to enforcement of major life-style choices. A social-worker emphasis among law enforcement personnel.	No change in level of crime.
Recreation More emphasis	Slight increase in expenditures across board. High demand for facilities.	In spite of demands for more, few local programs, except for elderly.	No major increase in activity; mostly a private-sector concern.	
Human services	Slight decline in local role as federal cash and direct assistance increase.	In spite of demands for more, few local programs, except for elderly.	Not a major local government growth area.	Exclusive concern of states and feds. Increase in programs for elderly.
Housing	High concern for adequate housing. Major private-sector role.	Deteriorating. Fewer single-family dwellings. Little localities can do, especially without private capital.	Less of a local concern, except for land use and building codes. Federal subsidies less; emphasis on encouraging private capital. Housing in good condition.	

New reformers: urban executives in the year 2000

Careful Village	Hope County	Doubt Town	Delight Community	Caution City
Elected officials/manager relations				
More separation of political and administrative. Managers more insulated from direct pressure from elected officials but more vulnerable to outside pressures.	Less acrimonious. More supportive. Shared responsibility for public and administrative matters.	Badly deteriorated. Low support for manager. Managers more tied to individual political leaders. Councils more involved in administrative matters. Patronage strong.	Reduced pressure on both. More supportive. More specialization, with elected officials dealing with public, managers with administration. Low profile for managers.	Deteriorated. Conflict.
The profession				
Manager as public leader. Tenure shorter, tensions greater. Technocratic specialization, brokering, intergovernmental contacts. Manager equity broker.	Fewer technical skills required. More of a broker, communicator, negotiator. Knowledge of current issues, human behavior, historical base of community. Demographically heterogeneous. Duties less rigid. More mayor-appointed administrators.	Fewer professionally managed cities and counties. Managers less involved in day-to-day matters. Key to management is politics rather than efficiency. People stay less time in profession; less mobile. Need skills in communications. Understanding urban economics critical. More managers assistants to mayors.	Need for more technically knowledgeable and managerially skilled profession. More a long-range planner. Support staffs more technically and analytically competent. Mobility continues, but security greater. Higher salaries. New form: strong mayor/administrator form with professional appointed by mayor and council.	Hard to find good managers. Higher requirements, lower security. Must be more flexible; change agents; brokers among factions. Skills in consensus building, economic theory. Most of the time spent with council and public. Very high pay, fixed term contracts. More "professional" assistants.

ICMA

Major national voice for local government. Political clout. Direct career support; regional offices, contract negotiation for managers. Membership difficult to attain; must be certified. Multimillion-dollar research program funded by ICMA Endowment. Dominance in urban research.	Merged with NLC, USCM, NACo, NARC. Continued needs assessment. No certification.	Broader membership, more political. Council-manager plan no longer preferred form. Ethics code replaced with more realistic statement. Most other associations for local government folded for lack of resources. Services targeted to support of managers in crisis and Washington advocacy.	Great demand for more technical and managerial assistance. Product and service oriented. Also midcareer development, personal counseling, and placement service growth. Emergence of two organizations: one educational and technical; other for personal service to individuals. Major support from ICMA Endowment.	Strong advocate and supporter of profession. Regionalized. Training shifted to career needs and personal concerns.

For further reference

This list includes works quoted in the text and additional sources of information on future projections, particularly as they relate to local government.

Advisory Commission on Intergovernmental Relations. *A Catalog of Federal Grant-in-Aid Programs to State and Local Governments: Grants Funded FY 1978.* Washington, D.C.: Advisory Commission on Intergovernmental Relations, 1979.
———. *Changing Public Attitudes on Governments and Taxes.* Washington, D.C.: Advisory Commission on Intergovernmental Relations, 1979.
———. *The Intergovernmental Grant System: An Assessment & Proposed Policies: In Brief.* Washington, D.C.: Advisory Commission on Intergovernmental Relations, n.d.
———. *Significant Features of Fiscal Federalism: 1976 Edition.* Washington, D.C.: U.S. Government Printing Office, 1976.
Alonso, William. "The Population Factor and Urban Structure." Working Paper No. 102, prepared for the Massachusetts Institute of Technology/Harvard University Joint Center for Urban Studies, 1977.

"Americans Change." *Business Week,* February 20, 1978.
"A Somber Forecast." Editorial. *The Washington Post,* January 27, 1979.
Barnouw, Erik. "So You Think TV Is Hot Stuff? Just You Wait." *Smithsonian* magazine, July 1976.
Bell, Daniel. *The Coming of Post-Industrial Society: A Venture in Social Forecasting.* New York: Basic Books, 1973.
Berger, Raoul. "The Imperial Court." *New York Times Magazine,* October 9, 1977.
Bezold, Clement, ed. *Anticipatory Democracy: People in the Politics of the Future.* New York: Vintage Books, 1978.
Boucher, Wayne I., ed. *The Study of the Future: An Agenda for Research.* Washington, D.C.: U.S. Government Printing Office, 1977. Copyright The Futures Group, Inc.
Boulding, Kenneth E. "The Anxieties of Uncertainty in the Energy Problem." In *Prospects for Growth: Changing Expectations for the Future,* edited by Kenneth D. Wilson. New York: Praeger, 1977.
Boyd, Marjorie. "Pensions: The Five

Trillion Dollar Scandal." *Washington Monthly*, February 1978.

Breckenfeld, Gurney. "Refilling the Metropolitan Doughnut." In *The Rise of the Sunbelt Cities*, edited by David C. Perry and Alfred J. Watkins. Beverly Hills, Calif.: Sage Publications, 1977.

Bronowski, J. *A Sense of the Future*. Cambridge, Mass.: MIT Press, 1977.

Brown, Harrison. *The Human Future Revisited: The World Predicament and Possible Solutions*. New York: W. W. Norton, 1978.

Bundy, Robert, ed. *Images of the Future: The Twenty-first Century and Beyond*. New York: Prometheus Books, 1976.

Burns, James MacGregor. *Leadership*. New York: Harper & Row, 1978.

Campbell, Alan K. "Metropolitan Regionalism." In *Urban Options I*, by National Urban Policy Roundtable. Alan K. Campbell et al. Columbus, Ohio: Academy for Contemporary Problems, 1976.

Churchman, C. West. *The Systems Approach*. New York: Dell, 1968.

Clem, Ralph; Greenberg, Martin Harry; and Olander, Joseph. *The City 2000 A.D.: Urban Life Through Science Fiction*. Greenwich, Conn.: Fawcett, 1976.

Cleveland, Harlan. *The Future Executive: A Guide to Tomorrow's Managers*. New York: Harper & Row, 1972.

Coates, Joseph F. "The Physical Nature of the American City in the Year 2000." *The Municipal Year Book 1979*. Washington, D.C.: International City Management Association, 1979.

Colman, William G. "The Future of Cities: Contrasting Strategies for the Haves and Have Nots." Paper prepared for the Conference on Reorganization, Woodrow Wilson International Center for Scholars, Smithsonian Institution, Washington, D.C., September 19–20, 1977.

Cornish, Edward, ed. *1999: The World of Tomorrow: Selections from "The Futurist."* Washington, D.C.: World Future Society, 1978.

_____. et al. *The Study of the Future: An Introduction to the Art and Science of Understanding and Shaping Tomorrow's World*. Washington, D.C.: World Future Society, 1977.

Council of State Governments. *The States and Electric Utility Regulation*. Lexington, Ky.: Council of State Governments, 1977.

Denison, Edward F. "The Puzzling Drop in Productivity." *The Brookings Bulletin* 15, no. 2 (fall 1978).

Dickson, Paul. *The Future File: A Guide for People with One Foot in the 21st Century*. New York: Rawson Associates, Inc., 1977.

Edison Electric Institute. *Economic Growth in the Future: The Growth Debate in National and Global Perspective*. New York: McGraw-Hill, 1976.

Finney, Jack. *Time and Again*. New York: Simon & Schuster, 1970.

Footnotes to the Future newsletter. Futuremics, Inc., 1629 K Street, N.W., Suite 5129, Washington, D.C. 20006.

Glendening, Parris N., and Reeves, Mavis Mann. *Pragmatic Federalism: An Intergovernmental View of American Government*. Pacific

Palisades, Calif.: Palisades Press, 1977.

Goodman, Percival, and Goodman, Paul. *Communitas: Means of Livelihood and Ways of Life*. New York: Random House, 1947.

Gulick, Luther. "Democracy and Administration Face the Future." *Public Administration Review* 37, no. 6 (November–December 1977).

Haworth, Lawrence. *The Good City*. Bloomington: Indiana University Press, 1963.

Hayes, Denis. *Rays of Hope: The Transition to a Post-Petroleum World*. New York: W. W. Norton, 1977.

Huston, Cynthia F., and Little, Dennis L. *Some Past Trends and Future Projections for the United States*. Washington, D.C.: Congressional Research Service, Library of Congress, 1977.

Hyatt, James C. "Population Figures Suggest Problems for Public Policy." *Wall Street Journal*, January 12, 1979.

"Innovation: Has America Lost Its Edge?" *Newsweek*, June 4, 1979.

Kahn, Albert J. *Theory and Practice of Social Planning*. New York: Russell Sage Foundation, 1969.

Kahn, Herman; Brown, William; Martel, Leon. *The Next 200 Years: A Scenario for America and the World*. New York: William Morrow, 1976.

Kasoff, Mark J. "Managing the City of the Future." In *How Cities Can Grow Old Gracefully*, Subcommittee on the City, Committee on Banking, Finance, and Urban Affairs, U.S. House, 95th Cong., 1st Sess. Committee print, December 1977.

Keesling, Karen. *The Year 2000 and the Prospect for American Women*. Washington, D.C.: Congressional Research Service, Library of Congress, 1977.

King, Norman R. "Economic Issues and the Future City." *The Municipal Year Book 1979*. Washington, D.C.: International City Management Association, 1979.

Kriken, John. "The Future is Here." *Mainliner* magazine, March 1979.

Levine, Charles H. "Organizational Decline and Cutback Management." *Public Administration Review* 38, no. 4 (July–August 1978).

Levine, Richard J. "U.S. Inflation Blamed on Attempts to Avoid Slumps, Aid the Needy." *Wall Street Journal*, June 19, 1979.

Martino, Joseph P. "Telecommunications in the Year 2000." *The Futurist* 13, no. 2 (April 1979).

Moffitt, Donald, ed. *The Wall Street Journal Views America Tomorrow*. New York: AMACOM, 1977.

Mumford, Lewis. *The City in History: Its Origins, Its Transformations, and Its Prospects*. New York: Harcourt Brace Jovanovich, 1961.

Naparstek, Arthur J. "Policy Options for Neighborhood Empowerment." In *Urban Options I*, by National Urban Policy Roundtable, Alan K. Campbell et al. Columbus, Ohio: Academy for Contemporary Problems, 1976.

National Academy of Engineering. *Telecommunications for Enhanced Metropolitan Function and Form*. Washington, D.C.: National Academy of Engineering, 1969.

National Academy of Sciences, National Research Council, Assembly of Engineering, Steering Committee for the Metropolitan Communications Systems Study of the Board on Telecommunications-Computer Applications. *Telecommunications for Metropolitan Areas: Opportunities for the 1980's.* Washington, D.C.: National Academy of Sciences, 1978.

Ostrom, Vincent. "The Third Century: Some Anticipated Consequences of Governmental Reorganization." *Publius* 8 (spring 1978).

O'Toole, James. *Energy and Social Change.* Cambridge, Mass.: MIT Press, 1976.

Perloff, Harvey S., ed. *The Future of the U.S. Government: Toward the Year 2000.* Englewood Cliffs, N.J.: Prentice-Hall, 1971.

Pettigrew, Thomas F. "Racial Change and Social Policy." *Annals of the American Academy of Political and Social Science* 411 (January 1979).

Ricklefs, Roger. "Cities May Flourish in South and West, Decline in Northeast." *Wall Street Journal,* April 6, 1976.

Schwartz, Gail Garfield. *Bridges to the Future: Forces Impacting Urban Economics.* Washington, D.C.: Office of Economic Research, Economic Development Administration, U.S. Department of Commerce, 1978.

Sherwood, Frank P. "The American Public Executive in the Third Century." *Public Administration Review* 36, no. 5 (September–October 1976).

Skalka, Patricia. "Farewell to the Youth Culture." *TWA Ambassador* magazine, April 1978.

Stillman, Richard J., II. "The City

Manager: Professional Helping Hand, or Political Hired Hand?" *Public Administration Review* 37, no. 6 (November–December 1977).

Stobaugh, Robert, and Yergin, Daniel, eds. *Energy Future.* New York: Random House, 1979.

Theobald, Robert. "Managing the Quality of Life." In *Prospects for Growth: Changing Expectations for the Future,* edited by Kenneth D. Wilson. New York: Praeger, 1977.

Thompson, Wilbur. "The City As a Distorted Price System." *Psychology Today,* August 1968.

Tolchin, Martin. "Intervention by Courts Arouses Deepening Disputes." *New York Times,* April 24, 1977.

Urban Futures Idea Exchange newsletter. Alexander Research & Communications, Inc., 270 Madison Avenue, Suite 1505, New York, N.Y. 10016.

U.S. Department of Commerce, Bureau of the Census. *Social Indicators, 1976.* Washington, D.C.: U.S. Government Printing Office, 1977.

Vail, Hollis. "The Automated Office." In *1999: The World of Tomorrow: Selections from "The Futurist,"* edited by Edward Cornish. Washington, D.C.: World Future Society, 1978.

Walker, David B. "A New Intergovernmental System in 1977." *Publius* 8, no. 1 (winter 1978).

What's Next? newsletter. Congressional Clearinghouse on the Future, 3692 House Annex No. 2, Washington, D.C. 20515.

Wicklein, John. "Wired City—U.S.A." *Atlantic,* February 1979.

Wilson, Ian. "The Changing Metabolism

of Growth." In *Prospects for Growth: Changing Expectations for the Future*, edited by Kenneth D. Wilson. New York: Praeger, 1977.

Wilson, Kenneth D., ed. *Prospects for Growth: Changing Expectations for the Future*. New York: Praeger, 1977.

Workshop on Alternative Energy Strategies. *Energy: Global Prospects 1985–2000*. New York: McGraw-Hill, 1977.

Wright, Deil S. *Understanding Intergovernmental Relations*. North Scituate, Mass: Duxbury Press, 1978.

Wright, Edward T. *Your City and the Future*. St. Louis: PSI Press, 1974.

Ylvisaker, Paul. "Some Political Difficulties for City Savers." In *Toward a National Urban Policy*, Subcommittee on the City, Committee on Banking, Finance, and Urban Affairs, U.S. House, 95th Cong., 1st Sess. Committee print, 1977.

Yates, Douglas. *The Ungovernable City: The Politics of Urban Problems and Policy Making*. Cambridge, Mass.: MIT Press, 1977.

Acknowledgments

The Essential Community was written by Laurence Rutter on behalf of the ICMA Committee on Future Horizons of the Profession. George R. Schrader, city manager of Dallas, Texas, served as chairman of the committee. Other members were:

Wayne F. Anderson, Executive Director, Advisory Commission on Intergovernmental Relations (ACIR), Washington, D.C.

Marvin A. Andrews, City Manager, Phoenix, Arizona.

C. T. Armstrong, Chief Administrative Officer, Regional Municipality Hamilton-Wentworth, Hamilton, Ontario, Canada.

Lawrence Bashe, City Administrator, Plainfield, New Jersey.

Alan Beals, Executive Director, National League of Cities, Washington, D.C.

Terry L. Childers, Assistant City Manager, Tyler, Texas.

William Clark, Executive Director, Urban League of Kansas City, Kansas City, Missouri.

Eugene H. Denton, City Manager, Wichita, Kansas.

Thomas G. Dunne, City Manager, Walnut Creek, California.

George H. Esser, Executive Director, National Academy of Public Administration, Washington, D.C.

John F. Fischbach, City Manager, Lake Forest, Illinois.

Frank Gerstenecker, City Manager, Troy, Michigan.

Lawrence Gish, City Manager, Stillwater, Oklahoma.

Alan N. Harvey, City Manager, Vancouver, Washington.

Norman J. Johnson, Professor and Associate Dean, School of Urban and Public Affairs, Carnegie-Mellon University, Pittsburgh, Pennsylvania.

Richard M. Kelton, DeLand, Florida.

Norman R. King, City Manager, Claremont, California.

John W. Laney, Assistant City Manager, Kansas City, Missouri.

J. William Little, City Administrator, Wauwatosa, Wisconsin.

Donald R. Marquis, Town Manager, Arlington, Massachusetts.

Robert C. Mauney, County Administrator, Richland County, South Carolina.

Chester Newland, Professor, University of Southern California, Washington, D.C.

Paul C. Nicholson, Village Manager, Western Springs, Illinois.

Christine Rapking-Allen,
Township Administrator, Township of
West Windsor, New Jersey.
Burke M. Raymond, City Manager, Gresham, Oregon.
Walter Scheiber, Executive Director, Metropolitan Washington Council of Governments, Washington, D.C.
Philip K. Schenck, Jr., Town Manager, Avon, Connecticut.
Wayne E. Thompson, Sr. Vice President, Dayton Hudson Corporation, Minneapolis, Minnesota.
Wayne D. Wedin, City Manager, Brea, California.
Robert B. Weiss, General Manager, Manchester, Connecticut.
O. Wendell White, City Manager, Hampton, Virginia.
Sharon Whitlow, Addison, Illinois.

Advisors and consultants to the committee were:
Guthrie Birkhead, Dean, the Maxwell School, Syracuse University, Syracuse, New York.
Kenneth E. Boulding, Institute of Behavioral Science, University of Colorado, Boulder, Colorado.
David A. Burkhalter, City Manager, Charlotte, North Carolina.
Richard Carpenter, League of California Cities, Sacramento, California.
Richard L. Chapman, Staff, National Academy of Public Administration, Washington, D.C.
Joseph Coates, Office of Technology Assessment, U.S. Congress, Washington, D.C.
Donald Dement, Communications Programs, Space and Terrestrial Applications, National Aeronautics and Space Administration, Washington, D.C.
Kennerly Digges, U.S. Department of Transportation, Washington, D.C.

Anthony Downs, Senior Fellow, Brookings Institution, Washington, D.C.
Thomas Downs, U.S. Department of Transportation, Washington, D.C.
Stephen Doyle, Office of Technology Assessment, U.S. Congress, Washington, D.C.
James Eberhardt, Conservation and Solar Applications, U.S. Department of Energy, Washington, D.C.
Kenneth Friedman, Conservation and Solar Applications, U.S. Department of Energy, Washington, D.C.
Arthur Goldsmith, Research and Special Projects Administration, U.S. Department of Transportation, Washington, D.C.
William Gorham, Urban Institute, Washington, D.C.
Robert L. Herchert, City Manager, Fort Worth, Texas.
Mark J. Kasoff, Associate Professor, Department of Economics, Antioch College, Yellow Springs, Ohio.
Gerald Kayten, Aeronautical Systems, Aeronautics and Space Technology, National Aeronautics and Space Administration, Washington, D.C.
Frank U. Koehler, City Manager, Scottsbluff, Nebraska.
James Kunde, Kettering Foundation, Dayton, Ohio.
George Lindamood, National Bureau of Standards, U.S. Department of Commerce, Washington, D.C.
Dennis Little, Congressional Research Service, Library of Congress, Washington, D.C.
Robert Maxwell, Office of Technology Assessment, U.S. Congress, Washington, D.C.
Selma J. Mushkin (deceased).
Richard P. Nathan, Senior Fellow, Brookings Institution, Washington, D.C.
Henry Nejako, Urban Mass Transit Administration, U.S. Department of Transportation, Washington, D.C.

John Osman (deceased).

John Richardson, National Telecommunications and Information Administration, U.S. Department of Commerce, Washington, D.C.

Richard Rowberg, Office of Technology Assessment, U.S. Congress, Washington, D.C.

Roy Saltzman, National Bureau of Standards, U.S. Department of Commerce, Washington, D.C.

Jewel D. Scott, Office of the City Manager, Kansas City, Missouri.

Joel Snow, Associate Director for Research Policy, U.S. Department of Energy, Washington, D.C.

Robert Theobald, Wickenburg, Arizona.

Francis Ventre, National Bureau of Standards, U.S. Department of Commerce, Washington, D.C.

David B. Walker, Assistant Director, Advisory Commission on Intergovernmental Relations, Washington, D.C.

George Washnis, Staff, National Academy of Public Administration, Washington, D.C.

Graham W. Watt, County Manager, Broward County, Florida.

Robert C. Weaver, Distinguished Professor of Urban Affairs, Urban Research Center, New York, New York.

York Willbern, University Professor of Government, Indiana University, Bloomington, Indiana.

...and others too numerous to mention.